Morocco

First published in Germany as *Im Labyrinth der Träume und Basare. Marokkanische Mosaiksteine* by Picus Lesereisen & Reportagen Copyright © 2004 Picus Verlag, Wien.

First published in English translation in 2006.

This first paperback edition published in 2016 by The Armchair Traveller at the bookHaus Ltd 70 Cadogan Place, London SW1X 9AH

English language translation copyright © Stefan Tobler 2006

The moral rights of the author have been asserted.
A CIP catalogue record for this book is available from the British Library

ISBN: 978-1-909961-25-8
eISBN: 978-1-909961-30-2

Typeset in Garamond MacGuru Ltd

Printed in Spain

Morocco

In the Labyrinth of Dreams and Bazaars

by
Walter M Weiss

Translated by Stefan Tobler

 ArmchairTraveller

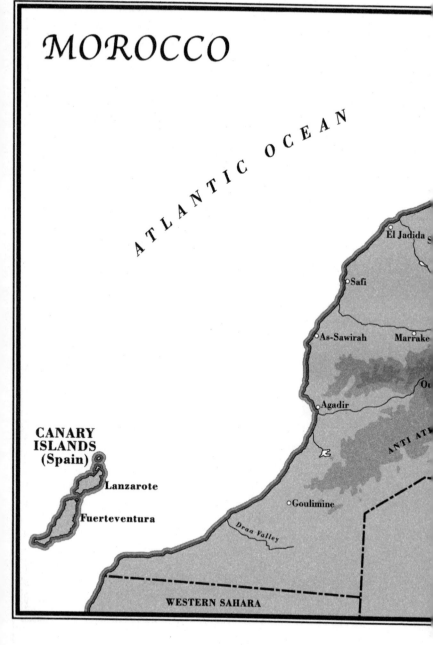

MOROCCO

ATLANTIC OCEAN

El Jadida

Safi

As-Sawirah

Marrake

Agadir

Ou

ANTI ATL

**CANARY
ISLANDS
(Spain)**

Lanzarote

Fuerteventura

Goulimine

Draa Valley

WESTERN SAHARA

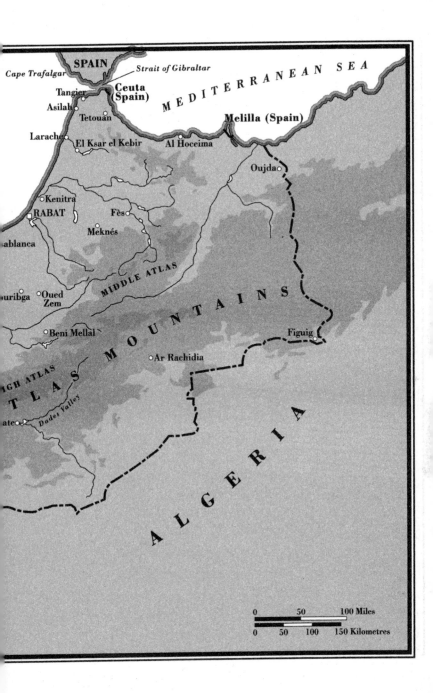

Contents

The Gateway to Africa   1

Coexistence in Morocco   9

Paradise in this world and the next   13

Hippy town and hotbed of resistance   19

First interruption: ça va?   23

Only look!   25

From the hammam to a full stomach, via hell   33

The healing powers of the dead   39

Second interruption: travel as a political choice   47

Trip to the edge of time   51

Moulay Ismail's legacy   57

Inside the bastion of power   61

Living and praying in the white house   67

Seaside snapshots   71

Among acrobats, storytellers and poets   81

An oasis of luxury and fashions   89

Barren lands and iron dogmas   95

In Hollywood's holy land   99

52 days to Timbuktu   109

Glossary   117

The Gateway to Africa

*Where Paul Bowles and
Noah dropped anchor*

Legendary places seem to require legendary founders. Several if possible, to suitably buttress their grand reputations. The ancient Greeks held Antaeus responsible for founding Tangier. It was said that this giant son of Poseidon and Gaia, the earth, created the first settlement on the amphitheatre of a bay at the north-western tip of Africa, and named it after his wife Tingis. Another legend ascribes the naming to Noah. When the dove flew back to the ark with clay on its claws, so announcing that land was re-appearing, Noah called 'Tinga'a!', meaning 'Land has come!'. And Hercules, too, had an indirect part to play in the town's founding. On either side of the gateway to the sea he raised the pillars of Calpe and Abila, today known as Jebel Musa and Jebel Tariq, alias Gibraltar, so creating the imposing backdrop for the later settlement.

Tangier, once called Tingis, has the longest uninterrupted history of settlement of any place in Morocco. It was influenced by the Berbers, Phoenicians and Romans early in its history, overrun by the Vandals and Visigoths, and at the beginning of the 8th century was conquered by the Arabs. Until the recent past it has been disputed by a number of world powers.

We are sitting on the terrace of the Café Hafa in Marshan, in the west of the town. Lemon trees, jasmine and bougainvillaea fill the air with the heady scents of a Mediterranean spring. Cicadas chirp and bees buzz. On the rickety table in front of us, a glass of scalding tea gives off the incomparable aroma of fresh peppermint leaves. At our feet lies the Strait of Gibraltar, brazenly blue and dotted with ships. An ideal place to celebrate our arrival and to ruminate on the curious fate of this important meeting-point of continents and seas, and on the Berber chieftain Tariq ibn Ziyad, who converted to Islam and in 711 led his trusty followers to conquer Al-Andalus, as the Arabs called Spain, after which it remained Muslim for the seven centuries until the Reconquista. And we remember two figures: Ibn Battuta, the Marco Polo of the Islamic world, who was born in Tangier in 1304 and set off from here to travel almost all the known world from Samarkand to Timbuktu, before returning decades later to die in his hometown; and Admiral Nelson, who defeated the Franco-Spanish fleet within sight of here, off Cape Trafalgar, to the south of Cádiz. The victory secured Britain's supremacy at sea for a long period. And we reflect on the longing that people on either side of this intersection between cultures are still assailed by: for the tempting, unknown other world.

We hear from Mahi, who has been openly puffing on a fat joint at the neighbouring table for some time now and is desperate to talk, that every year thousands and thousands of emigrants pay local fishermen exorbitant fees to smuggle them to Spain on moonlit nights. It is only nine miles away. Many of them are black Africans from who knows where. Quite a few drown when their boats capsize in the dangerous currents. Most are caught by the border police just before they reach their goal. Mahi asks if we've ever been to Ceuta or Melilla? In their two Moroccan enclaves the Spanish have recently erected miles of wall, protected by barbed wire, searchlights and thermal cameras. Yet the stream of refugees heading for the promised land of Europe is still increasing, we are told. In 1987 Morocco had applied for European Union membership and received a polite no as an answer. Another dream may become reality sooner. At the end of the nineties drilling work was started on a thirty-mile-long road tunnel that should – *inshallah* – connect Cap Malabata to Spain's Punta Paloma in the foreseeable future.

On the other hand, the Maghrib has been coveted in the West for a very long time – in different circumstances, admittedly. As so-called protecting powers the Portuguese, English, Spanish and French had a foot in the 'gateway to Africa' for centuries. Merchants from Genoa, Venice and Marseilles, as well as bankers from Paris and London, did business with Morocco. The exotic sensuality of the port town also attracted hordes of artists. Eugène Delacroix and later Henri Matisse fell under the spell of its light and colours. Antonio Gaudí was inspired by the earthy Berber architecture, and Camille de Saint-Saëns by its weird tones and rhythms. Writers like Edmondo de

Amicis and Pierre Loti in the 19th century ensured that Tangier had a literary presence as the setting for novels.

Its most glittering era began in the twenties, when the colonial powers who were fighting over this strategically important town managed to reach a compromise. They gave it the unusual status of an international zone. Taxes were abolished and nor were there customs or currency controls. The town was ruled by an assembly made up of nine Moroccans and 21 representatives of nine European states. Its 70,000 inhabitants – not a tenth of its present population – came from far and wide. They listened to *Pan American Radio*, which at the time was the only commercial radio station in the world to broadcast daily in six languages: Arabic, French, Spanish, English, Italian and Hindi.

However, the unregulated economic freedom did not attract only honest traders. Swarms of profiteers, prostitutes and black marketeers arrived, and spies whose role, it seems with hindsight, was largely to keep each other in check with a supply of rumour and intrigue. Tangier became a flourishing den of iniquity whose cosmopolitan flair had an irresistible attraction for bohemians too, especially those from puritanical America. Visitors included Tennessee Williams, Truman Capote, Gore Vidal and, inevitably, Gertrude Stein, as well as Evelyn Waugh, Albert Camus, André Gide, Joseph Kessel, Paul Morand, and the beat authors Allen Ginsberg, William Burroughs and Jack Kerouac. They all came, drawn by the promise of exotic impressions, alluring boys, and *kif*, the abundant local hashish. But sooner or later they all left to recover from their excesses, perhaps even having been cured of many a florid Eastern fantasy.

The only one who stayed, and who until shortly before his death in November 1999 would be seen now and then drinking a glass of mint tea in Hafa, was Paul Bowles. The great chronicler of Tangier's legendary past, he arrived here in 1931 for the first time, at that point still a composer. Ten years later he settled in Morocco for good and wrote the novels that brought him worldwide fame, such as *The Sheltering Sky*, later filmed brilliantly by Bernardo Bertolucci. He also researched the Berber peoples' musical traditions, as he travelled the land with a tape recorder in his hand. Why did he stay? He once wrote that North Africans were at peace with themselves, content with their lives. They were satisfied because they didn't ask questions. They were calm, not driven. The American dream, he added, was the dumbest drug.

A pale reflection of those decadent, international years still lingers in some corners of this overcrowded town, whose outskirts could now be those of any town. When we have a *café au lait* on the Place Mohammed V in the Café de Paris where *tout Tanger* once met, we find that a good number of tables are occupied by elderly gentlemen – pale Europeans with graceful gestures and overly white linen suits. In their practiced boredom they seem oddly distant from the present, enmeshed in old, velvety dreams. And the indefatigable Rachel Muyal in her small, nicely cluttered Librarie des Colonnes on the Boulevard Pasteur, where she has kept who knows how many literary legends supplied with reading matter, is holding the fort for a fifth decade. A few hundred yards further on, Adolpho de Velasco, the doyen of Morocco's art and antiques dealers, still runs the shop where his clientele, without a financial care in the world, come for more deliveries of artfully carved chests, expensive brass lamps, antique faience and glossily painted mirrors.

Most of the old hotels down at the beach are also still standing. We discover the Cecil, where Michel Foucault would put himself up, and the Solazur that Samuel Beckett preferred, the Rif, the Continental, and across from the train station the bizarre Gothic pile Renschausen, where the world-weary protagonist Port (played by John Malkovich) stayed in *The Sheltering Sky*. A handful of that age's evening sanctuaries also still exist: Guitta's Restaurant, for example, Marquis and Negresco. You could even imagine that a few stranded exiles sit among their grey-haired customers – shrivelled colonial officers perhaps, reprobate sons of millionaires, SS thugs in hiding or Vichy collaborators. All of these haunts, and the run-down villas of the Europeans in Marshan and Vieille Montagne, are irrevocably of another time.

The bar of the El Minzah, the most exquisite hotel on the square, still conjures up the sophisticated past. It did, after all, serve as the model for Rick's Café in *Casablanca*. But recently an extra storey was added to the distinguished establishment and the proprietors have already had cause to regret the expansion, because it hasn't led to the hoped-for increase in guests. It is not by chance that no investors have been found for the desolate grand hotel Villa de France, where Matisse once painted a number of masterpieces. Southern Morocco, Marrakech, the Atlas mountains and the desert have replaced the north as destinations for tourists and adventure-seekers. 'An unloved woman, seduced but not understood, forgotten by her lovers,' as the author Tahar Ben Jelloun, who was born in Fès and became famous in France, described Tangier a few years ago in an essay that he titled 'Le grand réveil', 'The great awakening'.

Coexistence in Morocco

Meeting the Jewish community

Tangier seems more authentic in its Arab heart – the medina. Its white cubed houses nestle picturesquely into the steep semi-circle of the bay. We wander from Gran Socco, the 'Main Market' where the *mendoub*, the Sultan's minister, once lived and where the area's Berber women still sell fruit and vegetables, through the Rue es Siaghin, once the Jewish silver merchants' street, to the Petit Socco. The beats liked to kill time in the seedy cafés of this little square. It is in the middle of the bazaar, which is small but lively, and obviously still a favoured location for shady dealings. Adolescent boys constantly hustle us in a whisper to buy foil balls of hashish. Mohammed Choukri, Driss ben Hamed Charhadi and Mohammed Mrabet were at home here and in neighbouring alley-ways. Their frank depictions of their youth as rent boys, *kif* smokers and pickpockets caused a sensation in the West.

We have an appointment with Moïse Bengio in Café Tingis on the Petit Socco. The friendly, elegant gentle-man, a retired merchant with business connections to

9

all five continents, had agreed the day before to show us Tangier's Jewish relics. A little later we follow him past the Great Mosque and the Spanish cathedral into a narrow alley, the Rue de la Synagogue. The poorer Jews, we hear, lived here in the medina, the richer ones in villas in Marshan. The synagogue is the first place he takes us. It carries the name of its famous builder, the Nahon family of bankers, and is scarcely 100 years old. In spite of that, it now serves as a museum. In the forties, Bengio tells us, the Jewish community here numbered almost 20,000. 'Many were involved in international trade and finance, many others were engineers, architects and craftsmen.' Today it numbers no more than 120. It no longer has its own school, just an old people's home. But at least the supply of kosher meat is still guaranteed by a slaughter-house in Meknès, and so the *kashruth*, the Jewish dietary laws, can be kept.

The first exodus from Tangier came in 1956 for both political reasons – Morocco's independence – and for economic reasons, as Tangier lost its special status. Further emigration occurred in 1967 and 1973, the years of Arab-Israeli wars. France, Spain, Canada and Venezuela were the emigrants' primary destinations. Only a minority went to Israel from Tangier. The second synagogue that Bengio shows us is only a little older than the first and similarly lacking in artistic interest, yet it does fulfil its intended role and provides spiritual sustenance every sabbath.

The old cemetery is our last stop on this walk into a hidden history. We wade through weeds up to our thighs and stumble on cracked gravestones. Our guide deciphers weathered inscriptions. Excitedly he tells us of the famous rabbis from Toledo, Fès and Córdoba who lie at rest here. Have we been to Chaouen yet? There, on the road towards Al Hoceima, Jewish graves can be found that are over a thousand years old! According to medieval manuscripts, Jewish families are said to have fled to the valleys of southern Morocco, on the edge of the Sahara, when the first temple in Jerusalem was destroyed. What astonishes us is that this enormous area – right above the city walls, high above the port – was apparently never seized upon by property developers.

'Jews had their set place in Moroccan society and were respected,' Abraham Azancote, head of the Tangier Jewish community, tells us the next day in his flat in the new town. Of course, he says, there were golden times and more difficult ones. But never, never were there pogroms in anything like European proportions. On the contrary, during World War II the Vichy regime ordered that France's anti-Semitic laws should be put into practice in Morocco too, but Mohammed V refused to do so. He said he was duty-bound to defend the Jews and couldn't allow any harm to come to them. And when he returned from exile in Madagascar, he stressed in his first speech that in Morocco Jews would have full citizenship, with all of its rights and duties. So it is not surprising that Mohammed V, who saved Jews from the Holocaust, is counted by Israel as one of the Righteous among the Nations. Nor a surprise that the monarchy enjoys a close relationship to Israel even today.

Someone who knows this 'special relationship' from personal experience like few others is Serge Berdugo, who has been the president of the Moroccan Jewish communities since the eighties. Morocco, as he will later expound to us in his villa in Casablanca, has long had an important role in the politics of the Middle East. As far back as 1968, King Hassan II was convinced that 'the sons of Abraham can live together without problems, if they find a *modus vivendi* that is based on mutual respect and dignity'. As a result His Majesty has continually tried to build bridges for a lasting peace. 'If one takes a cursory glance at the history of the Middle Eastern conflict since the Six Day War,' says Monsieur Berdugo in the polished French that he picked up as a law student in Paris, 'one can see that Morocco was involved in all major decisions.' As evidence he proudly pulls a folder from the drawer of his solid mahogany desk. *Voilà*, proof of more than 30 years of diplomatic wrangling. The thick bundle contains press clippings and photos of various delegations, summit openings, press conferences, and the well-known protagonists of the eternal drama: Yasser Arafat, Yitzhak Rabin, Shimon Peres and Bill Clinton. There in the middle of them, always their host in Rabat: His Majesty King Hassan II.

Paradise in this world and the next

Encounters with potheads, beatniks and gnawa

Happy hour at a café on the Boulevard Pasteur: watching the flow of people strolling up and down is like attending a seminar for applied sociology. The contemporaneity of non-contemporary aspects is, we could venture to say, just what every European finds fascinating in this country. Teenagers in skintight jeans, with bright red lipstick, parade arm in arm, cheekily making eyes. Blind old men beg for baksheesh with throaty calls, their bony faces hidden deep in the cowls of their gowns that look like monks' habits. Boys no older than eight wander from table to table offering cigarettes or to polish people's shoes, while in the apparently never-ending column of cars there will always be a driver with gel in his hair, a gold chain around his neck and a wide smile, ostentatiously revving his Mercedes' or Chevrolet cabrio's large motor.

More cannabis is grown in the Rif mountains to the south-east of the town than anywhere else in the world. Over three thousand tonnes, according to the latest EU estimates, make their way from here to the European markets every year: more than from any other country in the world. The region and Tangier don't do badly from it. Those in the know jokingly call the hundreds of blocks of flats and offices that have sprung up on the edge of town in the last two decades, and to a large degree are still empty today, the 'immeubles de la menthe', 'the mint buildings'.

The contrast between rich and poor is as wide in the medina. At every entrance unemployed men wait for good-natured tourists and offer themselves as guides. Sometimes they are boldly overfamiliar, sometimes – and just as irritatingly – fawning. This time even we let ourselves be hooked. Now escorted, we roam through the labyrinth of alleys, steps and squares that slope down below the Kasbah. It is strange how a middle-aged man without any prospects of a career can speak about the rich and famous so completely without animosity, even appreciatively. Malcolm Forbes, Brian Jones, Marguerite McBey ... As a child he saw them all. Yussuf, our self-proclaimed Cicerone, leads us to a brass-covered door. The palace behind it once belonged to Barbara Hutton, the legendary Woolworth heiress. The parties that she threw on the wide terraces are legendary and the more notorious of them attracted exaggerated headlines in the British and American press. 'What do these foreigners know of Morocco?' asked Mohammed Choukri in his autobiography *For Bread Alone*. 'They have used the city,' he says with the ruthlessness that street life teaches you, 'sucked it dry, like a lemon. Parasites, they come to whore and get stoned.'

Our next stop is the Old American Legation, another attraction for a nostalgic elite. In 1776 Morocco was the first country to recognise US independence. A little later the sultan gave this property to the United States. It was the young country's first foreign outpost. A museum is now housed in its extensive, elaborately decorated rooms. Thor Kuniholm, its director, shows us some of the highlights of the museum's collection: a Kokoschka sketch, works by Cecil Beaton and Yves St Laurent, engravings (several by David Roberts) and maps of Morocco (the best by Mercator, Ortelius and Leo Africanus).

In one corner of the Mechouar, the large square in front of the Sultan's palace where condemned criminals used to receive their bastinados before landing in prison, a snake-charmer is squatting. When tourists approach he lifts the lid of a wicker basket and blows a short, melancholy tune on his *ghaita*, the Arab oboe. This coaxes his toothless cobra to wobble its tired head, and brings the pitying public to part with a few dirhams.

On a nearby panoramic terrace our view sweeps across the harbour. How many persecuted people in World War II dreamed of reaching this place, or Casablanca or Lisbon! On a cliff in the foreground York Castle towers above the city. Its style is a mixture of Portuguese and Moorish influences, but it was built in the 17th century by a British governor as a symbol of his power. It has been one of Tangier's landmarks ever since. At present it belongs to Hubert de Givenchy. He, however, is not allowed to live in it, as it has been declared unsafe. The battlements facing the sea have cracks you could fit your whole arm into. Undermined by wind and rain, they threaten to collapse onto the beach below. In Marshan at the western end of the beach lies a villa in much better condition; it was the home of the late American billionaire, publisher and Arabist Malcolm Forbes. The museum that the eccentric American created in the house is disappointing. A handful of historical photographs, posters, documents and clumsily-made dioramas in which the master of the house, a passionate collector of tin soldiers, recreated important battles of world history. The snow white, neo-Moorish palace and its expansive, perfectly kept garden on a cliff above the sea are, however, magical. No wonder that it has even been used as a location for one of James Bond's adventures.

The next day a tour takes us to the Mechouar again. It is already dark and, drawn by curious sounds, we end up in a tiny space, open on one side towards the square. Three musicians are stretched out on carpets having a jam – or is it a séance? One is clapping on a tambourine; the second is clicking metal castanets with remarkable regularity; the third is plucking a *gembri*, a three-stringed lute. They lay a tuneful, strongly rhythmic singsong on top of their accompaniment. Three more men – the audience – clap along. They seem to be miles away already. We are invited to sit down. Tea is offered. The music, that had at first seemed rather a cacophony, is beginning to impose a strong suggestion on us. Its energetic syncopation is particularly powerful. In a break in the music we hear that the trio tours Europe sometimes as Gnawa Express. Great reviews from European newspapers are pinned on the wall behind them.

Gnawa music has its roots in sub-Saharan Africa – in Ghana, Mali and Nigeria. Centuries ago (the exact period cannot be ascertained), the Gnawa were brought to Morocco as slaves. Their descendents held onto their spiritual inheritance in the form of dances and religious songs in various Sufi orders. Tourists are most likely to know gnawa music thanks to the group on Marrakech's Jemaa el Fna square, that performs acrobatics to the rhythms of African drums for baksheesh. The magical and occult dimension is, of course, barely visible in that setting.

Brion Gysin, the writer and friend of Burroughs and Bowles, claimed that Morocco's music almost converted him to Islam. In particular, he was impressed by the ecstatic sounds that the mystical brotherhoods danced to. He didn't convert. But he did acquaint the Rolling Stones with the country's ancient village music, which led to a record (*The Pipes of Pan at Jajouka*). Jimi Hendrix and Ornette Coleman, and more recently Pharao Sanders and Randy Weston, also fell under the influence of masters of the *ghaita, gembri, darbuka* (tambourine) and *nira* (a wooden flute), the *oud* (a lute), *qanum* (a zither) and the *rebab* (a single-stringed fiddle). Even so, their passion for the music didn't lead to their conversion either.

Hippy town and hotbed of resistance

Tetouan and Chaouen: home to stoners and to Rif warriors

Our first trip across country, and we are starting to see the logic of the word 'chauffeur' having the same etymology as the French word 's'échauffer' (to get worked up). It isn't that the condition of the roads leaves a lot to be desired. Rather that some drivers display an admittedly charming, yet also frightening carelessness. Local bus drivers in particular seem to have wiped the right-hand driving law from their memory and to have made their own peace with God.

We are travelling south-east on the main route that the smugglers use to reach Tangier with their hashish from the mountains and their black market goods from the Spanish enclaves of Ceuta and Melilla. What a contrast this is to Tangier! Jacket and tie are exotic apparel here. Everywhere you look you see burnouses and jellabas. French is almost a foreign language and only for a well-to-do minority is the car an alternative to the mule or donkey. The road is lined with Berber women selling pottery, honey, sheeps' cheese and embroidery. With their wide brimmed, tassled straw hats and brightly coloured woollen clothing, they look almost as if they've just arrived from the high plains of Bolivia or Peru.

Tetouan was long home to pirates. Later it was the capital of the Spanish zone. It is even more of a hybrid than Tangier. The Place Hassan II and the surrounding streets are as Spanish as in any town across the Strait of Gibraltar. Their façades are decorated with faience tiles and their balconies with intricate wrought iron. The neighbouring medina, however, is enchantingly Eastern and is still largely encircled by a high wall. Its alleyways are a narrow, twisting labyrinth; the walls of its houses are tall, almost windowless and – in contrast to the inner courtyards – completely lacking in any decoration. The bazaar is said to be the country's third largest; only those at Fès and Marrakech are bigger. The bustling throng turns out to be on a pilgrimage of the senses. We get lost temporarily in the crowds. The craftsmanship here, especially of the potters and tailors, is held in high esteem beyond local borders. There is also a considerable Jewish heritage in the town. It is not by chance that the town was long called 'little Jerusalem', after many Jews settled here who had been driven out of Spain in 1492. Tetouan's name means 'open your eyes!' in Berber. If you head south out of town and look back at it a mile further on, you understand the command. Lying as it does on a plateau that forms part of the foothills of the Rif, its setting is unquestionably picturesque. Just under an hour down the road south of Tetouan, the town of Chaouen is even more beautiful.

This little town of 30,000 inhabitants lies in a saddle between two towering peaks and is surrounded by thick forests. Its sprawling medina is particularly appealing. Its low, gabled houses have red tiled roofs that remind one of southern Europe. Their walls, and even some of the courtyards and narrow alleys, are whitewashed to protect people from the heat and from insects.

Every few steps we discover small underground workshops where men are weaving textiles, cutting kaftans and making *babouches*, the pointy, normally saffron coloured leather slippers that are so popular all over Morocco. By many houses boys have hung up sheep's wool thread and agave fibres that they spin into yarn with little electric motors. Others sell semolina pudding sprinkled with cinnamon on engraved trays. Younger boys have fun rolling metal wheels, that they have loosely attached to their sticks with wire, through the streets. On the eastern edge of the old town a group of women wash their laundry in the ford of a stream. Time seems to have stopped in this mountain town that until 1920 no Christian was allowed to enter. Arriving at the main square, the cobbled, tree-lined Place Outa el Hammam, we suddenly feel transported to the seventies. For not only do tourists, their porters and local strollers congregate here, but also hippies – cooking under the midday sun, with their long manes, loose batiks and conspicuously slow gazes. In the numerous open air cafés the fresh mountain air mixes with the unmistakable sweet scent of hashish.

The neighbouring Kasbah was erected by a Berber sharif in the late 15th century as a bastion against the advancing Europeans. Within its reddish, earthen ramparts the cell can still be seen where the legendary rebel leader Abd el Krim was imprisoned in 1926. Still a hero to Moroccans today, it was here in the western end of the Rif mountains that he proclaimed an independent, Islamic republic of Berber tribes three years after he had started the Rif uprising. It proved to be a precursor to the later countrywide liberation movement. His French and Spanish opponents, however, defeated him with the help of a 250,000-strong army and the most modern weapons of war, including aerial bombardment and poison gas. It is no coincidence that Chaouen was the last of Morocco's towns to fall under the Europeans' influence. Even today the Rif Berbers are considered to be by far the most difficult subjects of the Alawite king Mohammed VI.

First interruption: ça va?

On the problem of the 'guides noirs'

Around three million foreign visitors come to Morocco every year. They spend more than ten billion dirhams (around 600 million pounds sterling) and are captivated by the variety and beauty of the landscape, the friendly and tolerant people, the climate and the unique, magical culture. What annoys everybody, however, and often casts a shadow over a visit, is the few thousand boys who – predominantly in the royal cities, Agadir and the main tourist traps – seem to view tourists merely as helpless, manipulable, infinitely rich, shopping-crazy idiots. They then often hassle the tourists so impertinently that not even strong words are enough to stop them. We aren't talking here about the honest, patient beggars, nor the crowds of laughing children whose sport it is to nick a *stylo* from a foreigner or to convince him to take a *sura*, a photo, of them. But rather the rascals who wait for the rental cars at the city gates and then pursue them to the hotels. The *guides noirs*, the 'wrong' guides, who latch onto their victims like burrs and, ignoring every polite and calm rejection, chat them up with ridiculous phrases from a variety of languages – 'Ça va? Amigo. Only look! Good price!' And not least the wannabe antiques dealers on the look out for a quick buck, who praise every piece of tat as antique and whose price is always a once-in-a-life-time opportunity. Even knowing that their behaviour is a result of horrific levels of unemployment and no doubt also cultural misunderstandings, unfortunately does little to ease the visitor's annoyance at their rudeness.

To their credit, the authorities have started to tame this crowd in recent years. In particular in Fès and Marrakech there is now a newly formed *police touristique* who ensure that contact is now considerably better mannered and more quickly broken off. Not that you won't be hassled at all.

Only look!

*In the maze of paths in
the Fès el-Bali bazaar*

In Eastern towns I like to follow Elias Canetti's advice. In *The Voices of Marrakesh* he recommends that you step onto a roof as soon as possible after arriving. There you can enjoy the view of the pure chaos down below that you will soon be lost in. When you look out over the landscape of flat roofs, he tells us excitedly, the whole town suddenly seems to be built of large steps. You think that you could walk across it. And the minarets, when the muezzins call, are like lighthouses inhabited only by voices, showing people where to go. In Fès I always use the roof terrace of the Hotel Les Merinides for this purpose. From there, this urban wonder of the world lies below, in all its incomparable charm, like a geode filled with a thousand precious crystals. Nor is there any better place to commit to memory the structure of the city.

Right in front of us is Fès el-Bali, the oldest and most thrilling quarter. There are two parts to it: Qarawiyin was founded in the 9th century by refugees from present-day Tunisia's Al-Qayrawan; on the other side of the river, the

Wadi Fès, is the district settled soon afterwards by exiles from Córdoba, appropriately called Al-Andalus. Further to the west is Fès el-Jedid, the 'New Fès' with its royal palace and *mellah*, or Jewish quarter, built 400 years later by the Merinids. And beyond that is the Ville Nouvelle, laid out by the French and spreading out more and more each year into the nearby hills. Rising on the horizon are the two 8,000-foot peaks of the Middle Atlas. Not in view, because it is behind us, is the youngest part of the town by far: a collection of unimpressive new blocks built as a substitute hometown for people from Agadir in the wake of the 1960 earthquake.

We weren't actually looking for a guide. We would have preferred to set off from Bab Boujeloud, the most beautiful of the city's gates, and wander, lost, around the bazaar's confusion of streets. But after a few steps and a short, most definitely unnecessary exchange of words, we find ourselves trotting humbly behind Muammar. The young man speaks polished French and broken English, and – in contrast to us it seems – he knows where we want to go. He steers us through the honeycomb of steep alleys and dark rooms, finding a way through the waves of people. In this seething mass of bodies, there's equality between man and beast. With the exception of a few streets, cars can't enter here, and nor does the present. Here too, as in all the bazaars between Marrakech and Samarkand, San'a' and Istanbul, the types of goods are strictly separated – both commerce and faith being well ordered.

We stroll through the alleys from one souk to the next,

from the weavers to the dyers, and from the saddlers to the tailors. It is a little like that scene in Fellini's *Satyricon* where the viewer is taken through a labyrinth of dark passageways, and doors open alternately to the left and right, revealing a kaleidoscope of strange images. Every nook of the shops, every workshop and basement displays a new, mostly bizarre, sometimes amusing, and almost always archaic scene. There are the comb-makers, who still saw each individual comb-tooth by hand from an ox-horn that has been pressed flat; and knife grinders who work their sparking stones by foot with lightning speed. Then there are the cobblers who cut white and saffron-yellow leather day in, day out, stitching it into *babouches*; the barrel-repairers and coppersmiths who were deafened long ago by the banging of their fist sized hammerheads; and, on the same shady, picture postcard square, the deliverymen with their mules and wooden handcarts. There are alpaca and scrap iron dealers, saddlers, embroiderers, carpenters, apothecaries, henna painters, women called *negafa* whose main occupation is to organise weddings, public notaries and clerks with their ancient typewriters, and a number of itinerant pharmacists and doctors who spread their leaves, roots and dried lizards out on the ground in front of themselves. They use anatomical sketches to explain the medicinal uses to illiterate passersby. Certain goods such as dishes, ploughs, leather saddles, birds, olives, honey, salt, and even snails, have their own markets. In short, if something can be sold, it's here. In the old city there are, says Muammar, about 800 different ways of earning a living manually.

Next he shows us a public bakery. Families bring their unbaked loaves of bread. Each loaf is given the family's personal mark and stored on long shelves. When the baker pulls the crisp loaves out of the shimmering hot oven on his baker's paddle, the notches avoid any arguments about ownership. Very close by is a *fondouk*, one of those hostels that traders visiting the city have slept in since the Middle Ages. In most Eastern cities such buildings are used for other purposes today – as warehouses, car parks or extra space for a shop. In Fès many still fulfil their original function. This 13th century *fondouk* has preserved the charm and appearance of that era. On the first floor spartan cells await guests behind colourful wooden doors. Most guests today are farmers who come to town to sell their goods and find cheap accommodation here. On the ground floor mules and donkeys doze between the columns of low arcades, tired from the long trek. Sturdy women squat over the earth floor of the courtyard, plucking chickens for the evening meal.

Standing in the middle of this hurly-burly that is always the same and yet simultaneously surprising, while a stork circles slowly above us, I realise what it is that makes Eastern countries so fascinating for us Europeans: people are anchored in their faith and happy to let the flow of events carry them through life. Of course, life's turns and changes are taken advantage of, but they aren't forced. 'We are transported from the highest to the lowest of worlds,' the writer Hugo von Hofmannsthal wrote in a foreword to the *Tales from the Thousand and One Nights*, 'from the caliph to the barber, and from the wretched fisherman to the lordly merchant. Its humanity lifts and carries us gently on its wide wave.' I can't help but remember the lonely Arab artists that are sometimes brought to European craft shows to provide a little ethnic colour, weaving, turning or hammering away for a clueless audience, as living examples of exotic craftsmen. In that situation they are touching relics; here in their hometown they are respected masters of their trade. Machines could produce a thousand times more than they do – but what for? Everyone in the medina has enough to live on. The social safety net works pretty well, efficiency is only expected up to a certain point. The men would rather have a chat with their clients, haggle and wait for customers. There is a fascinating contrast, as they know, between the openness with which they show strangers their wares and explain how they were made, and the privacy which they maintain for their houses, mosques and women.

In the Fès medina, crafts are again a profitable business. Over half of its inhabitants live from them and the number continues to rise. For it is now good form among Casablanca or Rabat's bourgeoisie to decorate a modern house with traditional materials such as *zellige* (mosaics made of glazed ceramic tiles), stucco, and carved wooden doors and furniture. More and more young men arrive from the interior, joined even by jobless university graduates, to attend one of the – believe it or not – 230 vocational schools, and to take advantage of the time to do a work placement too. This training is subsidised by the government. Diplomas from Fès have an excellent reputation and whoever has one will never be unemployed.

Being thirsty, we order tea in a small, dingy café. At the back of the café old men with grey beards and just as grey kaftans are sucking conspiratorially on giant water pipes. The pipes are available in such cafés for anyone to hire for a handful of dirhams. The water gurgles, clouds of smoke fill the air and the cool mint slides down our throats.

'Are you a believer?' asks Muammar, shaking us out of our agreeable lethargy. 'If you aren't, you will never understand Fès. This city is mysterious. Marrakech is a woman offering herself to you, garish and carefree. Fès though ... Fès is a veiled woman. She is difficult to win, but if you do, she won't let you go.' And then Muammar begins to tell us about its changing dynasties: the Fatimids, Almoravids, Almohads, Merinids, Saadians and finally the Alawites, who have controlled the city and country since 1667. And about the colonialists, who might have moved the court to Rabat and exiled Mohammed V, the grandfather of the present monarch, to Madagascar, but who never broke the resistance of the *Fassis* – the people of Fès whose families have lived there for many generations, people known throughout Morocco for their urbane culture and refined thinking. Then he tells us of the wild cheering when the French left the city in 1956; of the earlier loss of the city's dominant role in politics and the economy to Rabat and Casablanca; of the occasional earthquakes that might shake the mansions but don't affect most of the medina's houses, because 'everybody lays his beams right against his neighbour's walls'; and of the quadrupling of the population in the Old City since independence. Around 600,000 people now live in the medina, in not much more than a square mile. The elite are moving to the Ville Nouvelle. Their mansions are being taken over by poor migrants from the country. With the population density increasing rapidly, the infrastructure is under severe strain. The fascinatingly complex fresh water and sewage system from the 13th century threatens to collapse. And the buildings are full of cracks. In 1980, UNESCO took on the challenge and declared Old Fès to be a world cultural heritage site, allocating hundreds of millions of dollars to save its buildings and structure. With the help of private sponsors a number of flagship projects, such as the Madrasa Bou Inania and the Fondouk Nejjarine, have been restored in exemplary fashion .

Back out into the crowds. The spring sun is beating down. Its hot rays penetrate the gaps in the roof of rushes. They provide only makeshift shelter. Muammar has promised something special. He turns in at a gate where thick black smoke is billowing out. He leads us down towards the source of the smoke, into a pit that goes further and further down. Suddenly the spectre of a person appears. He is a black colossus, and here even his teeth have been blackened by soot. He welcomes us. His muscled arms throw more boards and timbers into the blazing fire that a pale, skeletal boy is heating with bellows. The two of them are the town's ember-makers. Early every morning they distribute glowing pieces of wood to the souks' locksmiths, silversmiths, cooks and barrel-repairers, who can then start their own, smaller fires.

It is not unusual to see black Moroccans. They are the descendents of the slaves that rich families kept up until the start of the 20th century. When the French finally banned slavery, most former slaves stayed with their old masters. Titus Burckhardt writes in his book on Fès that is as sensible as it is poetic, that 'slavery can be seen historically as a consequence of the nomadic and semi-nomadic peoples' war laws. It wasn't possible for them to keep captured enemies in camps. If the prisoners were not ransomed by their relatives, they were kept as slaves of their new masters until they could earn their freedom or until their master gave them their freedom. In the Koran and the Sunna this is seen as particularly pleasing to God and is a suitable way to atone for various failings. The slave was never merely 'an object'; if a slave was treated unfairly, he could demand of a judge that his master sell him. He was to be regarded as a person. His position as a slave did not cancel out his humanity, as all people are 'slaves of God'. It was only later, as urban culture developed, that the seizing of slaves in sub-Saharan Africa became a desired end in itself, and the war of faith only the pretext. As the Islamic way of thinking does not allow contempt for any race, in Islamic countries slavery never took on the brutal character that it had in ancient Rome or even in the 19th century in the South of the United States.'

From the hammam to a full stomach, via hell

A pilgrimage of the senses into the innermost part of Fès

We've headed for the hammam first thing in the morning. Stretching out on the slippery, stone topped platforms, we await the highly praised torture. A quiet groaning rises from the neighbouring niches. Two men squat beside us. They wear only loincloths, greet us in a friendly manner, and yet they are still torturers. One leans over me, grabs my limbs one by one and kneads them. When every fibre in my body has been squeezed and pulped, his assistant starts to scrub my chest, stomach and back with a rough glove that he's dipped in soapy water. It feels as if he is rubbing quartz sand into my skin. He regularly pours ice-cold water over me from a tin bowl.

After this exhausting procedure we catch our breath on a stone bench in this tiled labyrinth. Our hot bodies have been wrapped in linen cloaks and our feet slipped into overly large clogs. We are given sweet tea. An endless whorl of lute music floats out of a cassette recorder. A musty, century-old vault arcs above us. In front of us a monster of an old oven lets off steam, hissing and groaning. Foggy clouds waft around us. In the distance you can hear muffled, throaty chatting. Now and then someone chortles. The world and its complexities are sliding away with our perspiration.

Arab baths, like this one at the heart of the Fès medina where the same rituals have been practiced over the centuries, have always captured the imagination of Europeans. The fantasy held that they were havens of utter relaxation and uninhibited pleasure. Like the harems, they were seen as a symbol of the supposed sensuous eroticism of the Levant. Reading certain risqué passages and verses from classical Arabic literature might well lead you to believe that vice flourished in the heat of these steam baths. But any assumptions that conditions resembled those in medieval Europe, where men and women enjoyed wallowing together in wooden baths, would be wrong. The sexes have always been strictly separated in the hammam. Some Muslim baths are only used by men or women all year round. Some are divided into two separate areas. In most, however, the same rooms are used by each group alternately. In many regions a veil is hung over the entrance during the women's sessions.

An afternoon in the baths is often, even today, the only chance for women in the traditional medina to meet their friends outside their homes. Here they can indulge in gossip and discreetly look for a bride for their own son among their friends' daughters. They can shave their armpits and pubic hair, as the Koran prescribes, and at the end of these ceremonies gobble up piles of sweets together, so embodying ever more their husbands' idea of beauty. Yet the belief that social pressures are removed in the hammam along with the clothes is mistaken. Chroniclers of past eras reported that women loved to exhibit their wealth here. The modern equivalent of this passion for finery is the habit women have of bringing their make-up bags to the hammam. Today they mostly contain modern cosmetics, but there are also all manner of pastes, ointments and perfumes, made according to old formulae. There is kohl, essential for the eyes, and *tfal*: clay mixed with orange or rose water and applied to the hair, as well as henna, the reddish powder that the hair is dyed with after using *tfal*.

Both bodily and spiritual purification are very important in Islam. As it says in the Koran: 'Believers, when you are about to pray, wash your face and your hands up to the elbows and wipe your head, and your feet to the ankles.' This 'little' wash is to be carried out at the five daily times for prayer. If a person is unclean, this ablution isn't sufficient. After sexual relations and most certainly before visiting the mosque on Friday, the whole body from the crown of your head to your little toe has to be washed. For this more thorough wash, the hammams stand waiting for believers in the old parts of towns. It is a set-up that meets social needs just as perfectly as those of hygiene. Naturally, the numbers of visitors they receive is constantly decreasing as ever more people have their own bathrooms – and televisions.

And yet – you can still find a few of these stone witnesses to a refined everyday culture in the historical heart of almost any Moroccan town. They are open to everyone, whatever his or her belief. Their pleasantly dim atmosphere is a world away from the puritanical obsession with sport in our bright swimming pools.

Fresh from our bath, we head to the Chouara tanneries. The men here look savage, as if they were captives in one of the inner circles of hell in Dante's *Divine Comedy*. Half naked, with blood-red thighs, they wade through the tiled tanks and soak the skins with bright dyes. Mules, those taxis of burden of which the medina is said to have thirty thousand, are continually bringing new hides for tanning. They come raw, having just been sliced off the sheep, goats and cattle down by the river, and they stink of death. Three thousand goat's hides and up to six thousand cowhides are dyed every day in Fès. Before dying them, they are left for days in a lime bath, then transferred to a water bath, to which sulphuric acid and sea salt have been added. Now softened, they are placed in a mixture of oil and tanning substances; chromium alum is normally used. In this city we find 30 per cent of Morocco's leatherworkers, organised into co-operatives.

Starting early in the morning, they work ten to twelve hours a day, six days per week. Because they stand in the vats all day, a man explains in a rare break, they can't get rid of the colour or the smell when they go home. 'None of us could afford to fall sick or to get injured. No one has any savings, let alone insurance. Most of us started working here when we were just kids – and we'll work here until we can't work anymore. It was like that for our fathers and grandfathers; it'll be like that for our sons.' The tanners and dyers are highly skilled at using channels with locks, which let the dyed water out and fresh water in. The most common colour is cochineal. Sometimes the water is mixed with indigo, antimony or dyer's thistle. Then the water turns blue, black or yellow. Once the dye has worked its way through the skins, they are laid out to dry on straw on neighbouring roofs, while the men again try to rub the pestilential stench out of their pores.

From the tanners it isn't far to the butchers, and fruit and vegetable sellers. Seen from behind, their shops are dirty and sagging, like all the shops in the bazaar. But the shop fronts are clean and luxuriously draped. If the university and mosque are the head and heart of the medina, the food area is its full belly. It is full of desirable goodies: towering arrangements of dates, cactus figs, nuts, pomegranates and a great variety of fruit from the region's fields tempts you. The freshest of okra pods, *feqqous* cucumbers, courgettes and aubergines are piled up. Strange sea creatures promise epicurean delights. In butchers' shops, sides of lamb and living chickens await their fate in *couscous d'agneau* and *tajine*. Unbelievably delicious cakes, crèmes and flans, often covered with syrup, will make your mouth water – and your bathroom scales quake. Balmy scents waft from herbs, including the ever present mint. And to sprinkle over the top: spice dealers sing the praises of their blossoms, barks and roots. The most exotic menu could be dreamt up here. And if you had planned not to buy a thing, you had better change your mind. Then you won't feel weak for giving in when the titbits that are offered as you pass make you hungry for more.

The healing powers of the dead

Searching for holy energy

In the twisting heart of Fès el-Bali we stumble across one of the fourteen gates of the Qarawiyin Mosque. It and the university of the same name were until recent decades the intellectual centre of the country. Around 860 Fatima al-Fihrya, the daughter of an immigrant from Al-Qayrawan, founded the mosque. It is one of the oldest seats of learning in the world, older even than the famous al-Azhar university in Cairo and the Zaytuna in Tunis – not to mention the centuries younger universities in Paris, Bologna, Oxford or Prague. Ibn Battuta, Leo Africanus and al-Bitruji (alias Alpetragius) all studied and taught here. Around 1400 the famous historian Ibn Khaldun was working at the university. His three-volume universal history was the first work of modern, rational history. And shortly before the turn of the millennium a certain Gerbert d'Aurillac is said to have learnt the decimal system here, with its Arabic numbers and that important nought, which, as Pope Sylvester II, he later introduced to Europe. As non-Muslims, we can't enter this mosque or any other in Morocco. A glance stolen through the gateway into the courtyard only makes us regret it all the more. Carried by ornately carved marble columns, its pavilions remind us of the Alhambra's Court of the Lions in Granada.

Only a few steps further on lies Moulay Idris II's *zaouia*, his tomb and shrine. He was the founder of Fès and is revered as a holy man. The streets all around are *horm*, holy, too. Wooden bars at head height stop unclean animals from entering and force pedestrians to bow down, signalling to everyone that they are entering a special area. In the right-angled streets of the *kissaria* that borders this area, many devotional objects are for sale – korans, candles, prayer beads and scents. All day the devout stream past. On the outside wall of the shrine pilgrims find a brass hole that they put their hands in; they throw in coins and hope that some of the *baraka*, the holy man's blessing, will rub off onto them.

It is important to distinguish two separates types of belief in Moroccan Muslims. There is the shariah: based on the Koran, this is the strict, official body of Islam's religious laws. Then there are the traditional beliefs that large swathes of Morocco's population are devotedly attached to; these have their roots in a 'pagan' animism that the Berbers wove into Islam, which had been imported from the East by the Arabs. The beliefs still play an important role today. Central to them is reverence towards those 'drunk with God', the *aguram* as they are called in Berber. These are holy men (and occasionally women) who have been granted special spiritual powers by God. These personal powers can – by laying a hand, or spitting on someone – be passed on from one master to the next, down the centuries. What started as the work of individual, charismatic figures soon – as with monks' orders in the Christian world – became a movement. This movement, called *tasawwuf* or Sufism, is still active today as numerous brotherhoods. Their devotees meet regularly and, led by a master, their sheikh, they carry out mystical rituals in order to come closer to God.

The whole of Morocco is covered with whitewashed, domed buildings, called *marabouts*. They mark where these wise searchers for God were buried or worked; they are considered 'holy' places and their spiritual energies are said to offer protection and help to solve all manner of everyday problems. With corresponding expectations people make the pilgrimage to 'their' holy person. And once a year a *moussem*, a pilgrimage followed by a feast, is organised in his honour. The centre of this magical web of energies, that both holds people captive and supports them, is Fès. This is due to the founder of the kingdom, Moulay Idris I, as Faouzi Skali explains to us. Faouzi is an anthropologist and the founder of the Sacred Music Festival that takes place in Fès every summer and brings together the traditions of the three great monotheistic religions. He is also a walking encyclopedia regarding the history of Sufism and of his hometown. We are told that Idris I, then still a refugee, was welcomed by Berbers here. He married one and had a son by her. His son, Idris II, then founded the first Muslim town on Maroccan soil, in a valley of the Wadi Sebou. As he laid the foundation stone for Fès he also said a prayer that is famous even today: 'You know,' he said to God, 'I am not building this

41

town out of vanity or the desire for fame, but because it is a place where you will be honoured. And a place of peace between those who live here.'

A good 500 years after those words were spoken, an amazing miracle occurred: the apparently undamaged body of Moulay Idriss II was found. This added enormously to the city's holiness and has meant that all the Moroccan brotherhoods have been represented in Fès up to the present day. 'Sufism,' Faouzi smiles, 'is rather odd. It has no doctrines and isn't particularly based on knowledge.' It is possible not to know anything about the exterior world and still to be a truly wise and holy person.

The enormous cemeteries circle the hills around Fès like a wreath. Muslim burial grounds, unlike Christian ones, are always open for new burials. The city itself is also dotted with nodes of holy energy. An old saying goes that 'there's not a foot of ground in Fès where a wise man hasn't lived.' The kingdom of the dead is stronger than that of the living. Early one Friday, the Muslim holy day, we climb up to the Bab Ftouh cemetery, that lies to the south of the medina. We are swallowed by a sea of white-washed gravestones, covering several hills. White is the colour of mourning in Islam. Many people are coming and going; some pray, others sing. A guide explains that, unlike in Europe, people don't bring flowers to a cemetery; they tie together little packages of bread, dates and figs, and hand them to poor people in the name of their dead relatives. And poor people give each other symbolic bottles of water on the same occasion. Burials always take place on the day of the death itself, both for Arabs and

Berbers. A body washer will read several surahs from the Koran, then wash the dead person's body with rose water and burn sandalwood for its sweet smell. The washer then blocks all the bodily orifices with cotton wool, so that no *jinn*, evil spirits, can enter the dead person. After the funeral people wear mourning for 140 days.

From the hillsides on the opposite, northern side of the town, the tombs of the Merinid necropolis shine across at us. Nearer to us threatening black clouds of smoke rise, as every day, from the kilns in the potters' district. And we see that incredible feature of many Eastern towns: the town ends abruptly with the medieval town walls and bucolic orchards and olive groves begin right on the other side of them.

Here in Fès we find what we had previously seen in Rabat's kasbah: students busy learning as they walk up and down in parks and squares. One evening we fall into a conversation with Azzedine, a law student. After an initial hesitation, he pours out his heart to us over many glasses of mint tea. Next year, we hear, he will finish his studies. But instead of being happy about it, he's worried about the future. For today it's not only illiterates and losers who could become unemployed, but university graduates too.

Around 300,000 young Moroccans finish their education each year – only a third of them finds a job. Among university graduates alone, nearly 200,000 are now unemployed. And why? The unions accuse rich Moroccans of investing in property rather than in the productive economy. It is certainly true that more businesses in Morocco are started by foreign companies than by Moroccans. Added to that, for years the state has been cutting jobs massively, under pressure from the International Monetary Fund. A further problem, Azzedine complains, is the corruption everywhere you look. Exam papers are often bought and teachers bribed. If you want a government position, you don't only need to know someone in high places, you also need sufficient money for bribes, the baksheesh. So employees have to beg, cap in hand. The quality of education, and people's belief in its value, is decreasing all the time. What's the point of going to school? people ask. The elite send their children to private French or American schools. Of all the school-age children, however, only half of them are currently receiving an education. Not long before his death in the summer of 1999, even King Hassan II himself brought up the subject of education in his televised address on the occasion of the Youth Festival – an admission of the urgent need for action.

The underdevelopment of the education system has led to a second problem. By the 1990s you could already read in the newspapers of unrest at the universities. In Fès some people were even killed. The *intégristes*, as the radical Muslims are called here, were always held responsible for the disturbances. Could Morocco become like Algeria? That is the worry that can be sensed in many conversations. The fundamentalists, it is said, had thought ahead, and had long been infiltrating society's most important spaces: schools, universities and the cities' deprived areas. Certain factions seemed able again and again to torpedo the educational system with strikes, demonstrations and exam boycotts.

'Morocco is the only Arab country never to have been conquered by the Ottomans,' a lecturer points out later. 'Although we were always strongly influenced by Africa too, Europe is very close to us. We can look back on a long history of religious tolerance. At the end of World War II there were 300,000 Jews living in our country, for example. Mohammed V protected them steadfastly from Nazi persecution until the end of the war.' We hear too that the long tradition of a more or less independent kingdom has meant that Morocco, particularly in the wake of the May 2003 attacks, has proved less fertile a soil for religious demagogues than Algeria, a country that was occupied by foreign powers for centuries and so forgot its cultural roots.

The kings have always played a central role. They have succeeded in preserving their religious and moral authority, as well their political power. As a sharif – one who claims direct descent from the Prophet Mohammed – whose dynasty has now ruled for over 300 years, the ruler is both *amir al mouminine*, 'leader of the faithful by the grace of God', and *malik*, king, and head of the modern state. When Khomeini took power in Iran in 1979 and a radicalisation of the Muslim world looked imminent, Hassan II was quick to take over the chair of the international Al-Quds Committee, whose declared aim is the liberation of Jerusalem (whose name in Arabic is Al-Quds) from the Israeli occupiers. Soon afterwards he established a Council of the Ulema, that is, of Islamic scholars, who advised him, and now his son Mohammed VI, in all questions of the faith; the council and their local representatives are a strong network of loyal clerics. Hassan II was a man of as many faces as he showed in the portraits on every wall: posing at times at prayer in a mosque wearing a burnous, at other times as a golf player, or as a statesman in a pinstripe suit. From his coronation in 1961 he was revered like a father by all his subjects – by the farmer in a Berber village just as much as by the Casablanca businessman wielding a mobile phone. In 1999 his son, thirty-six at the time, took up the role seamlessly, filling it naturally with his own personal character, that of a young monarch at the beginning of the third millennium.

Second interruption:
travel as a political choice

Answers to a moral dilemma, using
Morocco as an example

When five bombs exploded on 16 May 2003 in Casablanca, not only did 40 people lose their lives, but the vast majority of Moroccans also lost some certainties about their country. The country's image of itself was shaken to its foundations. Until then they had imagined themselves immune to the violent version of Islam and its foreign influences – protected as they were by the centuries'-old tradition of a tolerant Islam and by the special status of their king, their political and religious head. It is true that alert observers had long warned, with good reason, that the enormous gap between rich and poor was the country's ticking time bomb. Any hopes that the young ruler Mohammed VI would, in contrast to his autocratic father, effect quick and lasting changes, have also been by and large unfulfilled. However, certain things are clear: the government and the king are, all in all, masters of the delicate balancing act between traditionalism and modernism, their foreign policy is moderate and pragmatic; parliamentary elections are fair, for the most part; there is a great cultural diversity; coexistence with the Jewish and Christian minorities is predominantly peaceful; and there are serious efforts to raise the status of women. In short, the country's elite is committed to the main tenets of Western liberality.

Since 16 May, that the Moroccans call their 11 September, everything has changed. Now a minority of obscurantist Muslims have revealed their intention to bomb a society that is in principle open, back into an intellectual early Middle Ages. This is a painful experience, as Egypt, Bali, Kenya and Tunisia can also testify.

As in those holiday destinations, the suicide bombers in Casablanca targeted the economy's mainstay: tourism brings more currency into the country than do money transfers from its emigrants or the phosphate mining. Indirectly, it provides around a million jobs. Its importance is also set to grow rapidly in future. As foreseen in a master plan with a budget of four billion dollars, by 2010 the number of yearly foreign visitors should rise from barely three to ten million, and the number of available beds from 100,000 to 260,000 in the whole country. Five giant seaside resorts are being built along the coast and expansive new hotel districts are being planned for the four royal cities. The options for more individual holidays are also constantly being widened, there is everything from walking and mountain-biking in the High Atlas, or camel tours through the Sahara, to golfing holidays and thalassotherapy. In view of these developments, the crude calculation made by the bombers and their henchmen is obvious: Western holidaymakers and investors will be scared off, the economy weakened and finally the political system itself destabilised.

The acute crisis, in the form of cancelled bookings and halted investments, was over in a mere three or four months. Yet more far-reaching questions remain. How is the terrorist threat to be met? Should travellers avoid countries like Morocco, indeed the whole of North and East Africa and the Middle East, in future? We should avoid simple answers. It isn't enough to brush aside the attacks as unfortunate incidents, relying on holidaymakers' short memory span. Of course the authorities took the necessary measures – such as raids, arrests and bans on preaching – and sentenced some to long imprisonment or even execution. In Casablanca hundreds of thousands of democratic people took to the streets to protest against the violence. And in order to reduce the extremists' medium-term ability to find fertile ground for their propaganda, suddenly – better late than never – social housing programmes and literacy campaigns were started all over the country.

Looked at objectively, you can travel in Morocco as safely as you ever could. An evening stroll in the bazaars of Fès and Marrakech is incomparably safer than one through many large European cities. Desert tours do not hide any political perils, unlike in neighbouring Algeria. And thanks to the effective work of the tourism police, even the problem of young people offering themselves as unwanted guides, so irritating in the past, is more or less under control. The real predicament lies elsewhere: in the subliminal fear that uninformed holidaymakers feel. The Islamic world is suffering from a loss of image.

A recent study revealed that more than half of tourists considered their personal safety as a more important criterion than value for money when choosing a holiday destination. It is self-defeating for tour organisers to ignore this. Rather, the situation demands openness and transparency. The best precautions cannot guarantee complete security for anyone, anywhere. This is all the more true in the present circumstances, where the wave of terrorism is not, we fear, about to dissipate but to swell. Yet why shouldn't a virtue be made of necessity?

The way we act as consumers, whether in the supermarket, at the furniture dealer's or at the petrol station, is now influenced by social and ethical considerations. Shouldn't the tourist industry's customers also be made aware of the implications of their holidays? Travel has lost its innocence. Every booking involves certain choices. And people who spend their holidays in a country beyond the Mediterranean Sea, are today signalling their rejection of hatred and fear. They are showing that they still hope for international understanding, and are open to the world and in particular to people who are making an honest effort to bring about progress and development.

Trip to the edge of time

Visiting Berbers in the Rif mountains

Our friend Abdellatif, a Berber from Fès, has promised to show us his parents' village. We drive northwards into the Rif mountains on the road that young volunteers constructed when Morocco gained its independence. It was a special project to open up this remote part of the country. The area is fertile and blessed by nature. Fields of wheat, maize and millet skirt the road and we sometimes pass very steep, terraced hills that are covered with olive trees. Almost every roof has a stork's nest. Again and again, we overtake women who are hauling home giant bundles of firewood, swaying under the load. In the fields, too, there are almost only women working.

At times we see *kif* plantations from the car. They shine lush green now in spring. In mid-summer, before the harvest, they will be yellowy green. *Kif*, as hashish is called here, is grown on over 300,000 acres. We sometimes pass road blocks. Uniformed men search the cars for drugs. 'Blocks that don't stop anyone!' our friend smirks. Policemen are paid terribly in Morocco and the roads into the Rif mountains are a popular place to work.

Shortly before Taounate we turn onto a dirt road. It is bumpy and criss-crossed by wide cracks. It looks as though this year, as so many recently, the rains won't come. Our friend's family gives us a hearty welcome. The girls kiss our hands shyly, as is the custom here. Then they flit to the kitchen to prepare breakfast. The head of the house meanwhile shows us the village. Fifteen families live here, around 150 people. Although the high voltage line that connects Fès to the coast can be seen from here, the settlement has no electricity. We can't even see any machines – no generator, vehicle, television or radio. Nor is there a postal service (the village doesn't have the requisite address) or a well. Twice a day the women have a half hour walk with cans and mules into the hills to fetch water. No one pays taxes here and a policeman has rarely entered the village since the state stopped forcibly recruiting young men for the military. Morocco now has an army of professional soldiers. People only need money for the weekly market, where they buy clothing, live-stock, tea and sugar. The community is self-sufficient for day-to-day life. Apart from the meagre yields of farming, the family's only source of monetary income is wood carving. Once a month a mule is loaded up and the wares are taken to the bazaar in Fès, 50 miles away.

Then we are introduced to the sheikh. He is elected by the villagers – both men and women – and is respected by all, including the young. This means that he can deal with most conflicts. The state judge is only needed in exceptional circumstances, for serious violence or traffic accidents. The sheikh has two wives, a third died recently.

Both wives live with their children in the very same living area. He also owns a donkey, a cow, three goats and many chickens.

Later we all squat on a carpet in the courtyard. The meal is absolutely simple and delicious: millet bread, olives, olive oil freshly pressed from green olives, and mint tea. The sheikh tells us proudly that he is sixty-two and has eleven children. A further five died at a young age. The causes? He doesn't know. Had they had vaccinations? They were too expensive and a waste of time. If a child becomes ill, it will die. 'Allah gives,' he said, 'and Allah takes.' Asked what his children hoped for the future, he mentioned that his daughters would soon be married. He didn't send them to school. Why should he? The boys declare that they don't want to go to the city, they want to stay in the village. It's nicer here, there's no noise, and no dirt. Here it's peaceful and they are happy, they say, beaming at us. In any case, who else could look after the old people? There is no health service or pension in the villages. The next generation is the previous one's insurance plan. Respect for the elderly is a bedrock of this society. 'A mother's pains in childbirth,' our friend reminds us, 'can't be made up for in a whole lifetime.'

His mother is about 70, Abdellatif tells us. He says 'about', because the exact date of her birth, as of many women of her generation, is not known. In many small, remote villages people haven't been properly registered by the authorities even today; often they don't have any form of identity. His father, by the way, is 104. He used to earn his money carving out wooden ploughs. And now

Abdellatif starts to talk more generally about the Berbers. He estimates that there are as many Berbers in Morocco as there are Arabs. The Arabs live mainly in towns. Broadly, the Berbers can be divided into three groups: the Shluh who live mostly as settled farmers in the western High Atlas, the Anti-Atlas, the Sous Valley and the southern valleys that border the Sahara; the Berabers who keep goats and sheep and live a half-nomadic existence in the eastern High Atlas and the Middle Atlas; and the Rif who are farmers in the mountains of the same name. He tells us of their varied features, eyes that are blue here and light brown or green there, of the face shapes that range from narrow to wide, even square. He also mentions the three main language groups. Tarifit is spoken by the Rif, Tamazight by the Berabers and Tachelit by the Shluh; and then there are the many thousands of Berber dialects that are often as different as German and Dutch, or Italian and Spanish. But what they have in common is more important to him. Traditional men still wear a turban and, in contrast to Arab women who wear a veil, women wear the *hendira*, a geometrically patterned, woollen cloak. Lastly he mentions the tattoos that almost every woman in the countryside has on her face and hands, sometimes on her neck and feet too. They are decorative, and also bring good luck and protection from evil spirits, in addition to being a kind of lifelong personal ID, revealing their tribe. Did we know that every family has its tattoo specialists? Mostly older women. They trace the pattern on the skin with a piece of charcoal or cigarette ash. Then they heat a needle and scratch the lines until blood flows.

They rub charcoal dust or antimony into the coagulating blood. There are, we learn, around 1,200 different designs and motifs. Among the Shluh, the men, too, often have a little tattoo on or near the nose.

And on our trip back to Fès an old chestnut is brought up in our conversation again: what is the cause of the relatively static nature of societies in the Islamic world? Is it the fact that there has been no intellectual renewal equivalent to Europe's Renaissance? Is it the absence of an Islamic Enlightenment? Is the West's superior weapon's technology and its consequent imperialism to blame? Titus Burckhardt has an answer here too. 'Islamic culture,' he writes, 'focuses on its spiritual origins, as the Christian culture of the Middle Ages did. In contrast, our modern civilisation looks to the future. When the origins of a culture are perceived as divine, then what follows cannot help but be a pale reflection of them. The world cannot improve. "Every century after this one will be worse than the one that came before," the Prophet said. Every devout Muslim knows this, and this explains why Islamic culture in its later stages is much less dynamic than Europe's rationalistic culture. In Europe, the pursuit of knowledge and technical progress is rated more highly than the search for eternal truths and their realisation in an individual's soul.' And he tells the story of a sheikh from Tangier who, when the Europeans brought electric lighting to his newly occupied town, remarked: 'If these people were forced to pray five times a day they would soon leave off such child-ish play.' And this says more in the end than any socio-political analysis, however clever it may be.

Moulay Ismail's legacy

Splendour and madness in Meknès

We visit the smallest of the four royal cities. Meknès
bears monumental witness to the need for ado-
ration that plagued Moulay Ismail, the second Alawite
sultan. For half a century this man, who was as much a
despot as a lover of grandeur, had tens of thousands of
slaves and prisoners erect a monumental palace here. At
its centre is the sultan's mausoleum, our first stop. It is one
of the country's finest pieces of architecture, and one of
the few sacred sites that we non-Muslims are allowed to
enter (with the exception of its innermost sanctuary). Its
outer courtyards and halls display a beautiful unity and
elegance. The room where the tomb is actually located is
decorated with fine mosaics, faience and cedarwood carvings, as well as two longcase clocks, looking rather out
of place here. They were gifts from Louis XIV. Moulay
Ismail saw himself as a kind of Moroccan Sun King. Not
only did he maintain trading relations with his contemporary and role model in Paris, he even asked him for
the hand of his daughter Anne-Marie de Bourbon, and

encouraged him to convert to Islam. Both attempts were, as you might imagine, fruitless.

We stroll around the rest of the imperial city too. Most of this enormous area, shielded from curious eyes by high walls, has been converted into a royal golf course. Thanks to Hassan II's passion for greens and holes, every Moroccan town where His Majesty stayed for any length of time now has such a course to show for it, with greens that seem to have been trimmed with nail-scissors. Passing the recently renovated main gate of the king's palace, the Dar el Makhzen, we reach the Heri es Souani: the storerooms and granaries. Moulay Ismail not only suffered from megalomania, he also suffered from paranoia. As well as his 500 harem women, by whom he is said to have fathered almost 1,000 sons, he possessed a 150,000-man army. In order to be able to feed them in a siege – which never actually occurred – he had these storehouses and stables built. A large part of the gigantic vault collapsed in the 1755 earthquake, which also left Lisbon in ruins. But the hundreds of remaining arcades of rammed earth columns and the water house with its 130-foot deep cistern are impressive sights in themselves. 12,000 horses and supplies for two years could have been kept here.

From the café terrace on its roof we can take in the whole complex. The fanatical ruler had three defensive walls constructed around his residence and the medina. They are 25 miles long and almost completely undamaged. Around the corner the Agdal Basin, a ten-acre water reservoir, has also survived. However, only sparse ruins are left of the 30 residential palaces. The most beautiful of the city's 20 gates is the Bab Mansour. 'Rosettes, stars, the endless intricacy of interrupted lines, unimaginable geometric combinations that confuse the eyes, like a visual puzzle, but that always bear witness to the most educated and original of tastes: all of this was woven together with a myriad of tiny glazed tiles that curved inwards and outwards, giving them from a distance an illusion of a cloth shot through with gold.' This was the writer Pierre Loti's impression of its effect. The marble columns that flank the colossal gate were taken from the nearby Roman city of Volubilis. From the gate we amble across the Place el Hedim, the central square that joins the royal city to the old city, and into the medina. It is pretty, and of a comfortably small size, but is nothing spectacular. Its jewel is the Madrasa Bou Inania, the old theological institute. Its harmonious mix of cedarwood, white stucco, and *zellige* of a discreetly muted colour, make it a typical example of Merinid architecture. From its roof we can peak into the décolletage of the whole district.

One of the country's greatest mystics, Sidi Mohammed Ben Aissa, is buried in the cemetery to the north-west of the medina. He founded the Aissawa brotherhood. Legend has it that its members have struck a pact with all animals. During their yearly festivals, the *moussems*, they not only walk barefoot on burning coals and splinters of glass, and pierce their cheeks and tongues with sharp objects, they also eat scorpions and snakes and imitate certain animals' behaviour.

What a magnificent sunset! We have driven north from Meknès for under half an hour, through rolling hills of olive groves and corn fields. We stopped off at Moulay Idris, a picture-postcard town on a spur of the Zerhoun mountain. It is where Moulay Idris, the founder of Morocco's first kingdom and father of the builder of Fès, lies buried. Consequently it is seen as the country's most important place of pilgrimage. Now we are standing in the ruins of Volubilis. The last tourist coach has just left. Only a few scholarly-minded individuals are still plodding through what is left of the walls or sit on the stumps of columns, lost in thoughts about history. Looking south to the horizon, the landscape is an endless sea of undulating fields. Only a few cypresses and pines frame the picture. Birds are chirping. The woolly clouds in the sky are turning red. The only thing missing in this perfect idyll is a shepherd playing a flute. And if it weren't for the triumphal arches, the rows of pillars and the maze of ruins, graves and even paved roads, no one would imagine that this bucolic emptiness was once the setting of one of Rome's most important bases in the extreme south-west of their empire.

Inside the bastion of power

Rabat – royal residence and gateway to the West

Rabat is Morocco's Ottawa, Berne or – less violent and cleaner – Washington DC. Its 1.4 million inhabitants make it Casablanca's little sister, but it has been the seat of governments and the location of foreign embassies ever since the French decided in 1912 that Fès, which had been the capital until then, was too rebellious. Rabat is the youngest of the four royal cities and is considered the most modern, greenest and chicest. Our first walk takes us to the Kasbah des Oudaia, a fortress built on a rock between the river and the sea, where Berbers had already built a fortified monastery (*ribat*) in the 10th century. Yacoub al-Mansour, the Almohads' great leader, turned it into the centre of his kingdom. He assembled his troops here, before loading them onto ships bound for Spain, where they conquered much of the land for Islam. The kasbah's current name derives from the Arab Oudaia tribe. Around 300 years ago Sultan Moulay Ismail, the builder of Meknès, stationed the tribe here to protect the town. An Andalusian garden graces the sprawling area inside the kasbah. Between its scented hedges and flowerbeds students wander, holding their lecture notes. There may not be much room, or peace and quiet, in their families' houses. Here they are free to revise for their exams. Rabat University has around 20,000 students, making it the country's largest institute of higher education. Sitting on the terrace of the neighbouring Café Maure our gaze can sweep over to Rabat's twin city, Salé, and down to the nowadays rather desolate mouth of the Wadi Bou Regreg. In the 17th and 18th centuries pirates set out from down there to seize trading ships all over the Mediterranean and even off the coasts of England and Newfoundland. The local corsair state of Bou Regreg, founded in 1627, became very rich for a time, thanks mainly to a flourishing slave trade and ransom money. And the punitive expeditions that the enraged, seafaring Christian nations undertook against the pirates' stronghold (and which even the distant Habsburgs participated in), were all doomed to failure, as their high-seas ships could not navigate the shallows of the river mouth.

In the palace and the kasbah's magazines two museum collections are housed. Valuable manuscripts, book bindings, carpets, pottery, coins and musical instruments are all on display, as well as costumes from various regions. Unfortunately the labelling leaves a lot to be desired, as so often in Morocco's museums. A woman sits in a niche by the main gate and paints henna decorations on tourists' hands for a small fee. Of course, it is a far cry from the work of the real *harquus* decoration that even today traditional women have painted on their hands, feet and even faces every few weeks. But she does use the real henna powder that is mixed with water and lemon juice, and she applies it in an intricate design with the *kalame*, which is like a little toothpick, drawing with a free hand and not, as so often seen, with the help of a stencil.

Here, too, in Rabat the juxtaposition of old and new, and of European and Arab atmospheres, is astonishing. The old city is comparatively small, but its crooked little streets and its many workshops and shops – for carpets, clothing, jewellery, leather goods and food – are wonderfully chaotic, as a medina should be. And yet only a few minutes' walk away, along the palm-lined Boulevard Mohammed V, we encounter an almost Parisian elegance. It is where the rich and beautiful while away long hours.

The government district, the Mechouar, is almost obscenely spacious. Its 135 acres encompass, in addition to the Dar el Makhzen (the royal palace), the offices of the prime minister and minister of religion, the supreme court, a mosque, a horse-racing track, a golf course, the Guard's barracks, and the Royal College where King Mohammed VI and his younger brother, Moulay Rachid, were educated. Around 2,000 people, a mixture of palace officials and members of the many branches of the royal family, live inside the high walls of this town within a town. It has a mysterious political aura of its own. Even though we outsiders are only allowed to see a tiny and harmless corner of the royal district on an official tour, the number of guards spells out the message clearly: every step that we take is being watched closely.

Our next port of call is at the city's landmark, the Hassan Tower. With his characteristic excessiveness,

Yacoub al-Mansour ordered the building of the largest mosque in the Maghrib, the second largest in the whole Muslim world. Its prayer-hall was to be formed of 20 aisles, carried on 400 columns, and was intended to be big enough for 40,000 worshippers, his whole army. The plans for the minaret specified a height of 265 feet, and were designed, as it happens, by the same architect as the Koutoubia in Marrakech and the Giralda in Seville. After al-Mansour died and the Almohad residence moved to Marrakech, the project was never completed. Most of the completed shell of the mosque collapsed in the earthquake of 1755. Apart from a few individual walls, only the half-finished, 165-foot high tower survived. Many of the columns have now been re-erected and the square has been laid with new flagstones. The nearby mausoleum of Mohammed V, the father of Moroccan independence, where Hassan II was also laid to rest, displays a rather more frothy pomp. No doubt about the lavishness of its materials: the sarcophagus is of white onyx, the dome is carved in mahogany, and the parade guards' weapons are inlaid with worked silver and ivory. On the whole, however, this monument designed by a Vietnamese architect called Vo Toan seems rather haphazardly eclectic.

To the south of the city walls, the Chellah provides us with quite a contrast to the well-kept display of authority we have just seen. It was on this site of the ancient settlement Sala Colonia that the Merinids built a necropolis around 50 generations after the Romans. The walled area of Chellah is magical. The ruins have largely been overrun by chest-high bushes. Storks nest on the broken tops of columns and in the weathered minarets. A colony of several hundred cattle egrets have made their home in the surrounding trees. Their ear-splitting screeching and the stink of their excrement, and of the many dead chicks, give the place a threatening feel in the heat of early summer. It is the tropics' smell of decay. By a *zaouia*, once a retreat for a mystical brotherhood, we discover a stone pool. In its shallow, murky waters, eels are swimming. We hear from an attendant that they are holy. They can bless infertile women with children, if the women light a votive candle in their honour.

Living and praying
in the white house

Casablanca – metropolis and monster

The conurbations of Rabat and Casablanca are only 50 miles apart and have a symbiotic relationship. One is the political and administrative head of the country, the other is the pulsing heart of its economy. If neighbouring Mohammedia is included, three-quarters of Morocco's industry is based in the greater Casablanca area and four-quarters of its export goods leave through Casablanca's port and airport. Over 50 per cent of Morocco's gross national product is created here. A century ago there were only 10,000 inhabitants in Dar el Beida, 'the white house', as it was officially called in Arabic until the Spanish version of its name gained general acceptance. Today there are three million according to official figures, and four million by some unofficial estimates. Not much remains of the 'colonial' atmosphere that was conjured up so expressively in the film *Casablanca*, even if it was all filmed in studios. In the velvety piano bar of the plug-ugly Hyatt Regency on United Nations Square, a handful of posters of Humphrey Bogart, Ingrid Bergman, Paul

Henreid and Claude Reins have been hung. Along the Boulevard Mohammed V, the Rue Prince Moulay Abdallah and a few side streets, rows of exquisite town houses have been preserved from the time of the great building boom in the 1930s. Their cupolas, towers, columns and oriels show a delightful combination of elements of art deco and art nouveau, and of neo-Moorish and neo-classical styles.

South of the city centre, the Habbous quarter, designed by the French in 1923, demonstrates that it is also possible to combine a traditional medina with modern town planning. While in the two rich districts of Anfa and beachside Ain Diab a good number of extravagant, architecturally interesting villas can be seen. The rest, sadly, blurs in the city centre into a faceless mass of reinforced concrete buildings, growing louder and taller from year to year, while the miserable slums on the edge of the city grow rampantly without any check. There are supposed to be 3,000 mosques in greater Casablanca, and that isn't counting the unofficial ones in the poor areas.

By far the most impressive of them is right by the sea and it is – not by chance – named after the former king. The Hassan II Grand Mosque is the largest religious building in the Maghrib. In fact, with the exception of the mosque in Mecca, it is the largest in the Muslim world. As a 'lighthouse for Islam' it shines the Prophet's light on Europe and America from its geographically extreme position on the western edge of Africa. As a monument to their ruler, it also makes the monarchy's unmistakable power and divine legitimacy vividly clear to Moroccans.

Yacoub al-Mansour, Moulay Ismail, Mohammed V ... the country's most important rulers all immortalised themselves as *grands bâtisseurs*, great builders. This mosque, dedicated in 1993, proved Hassan II to be an heir worthy of his Alawite dynasty, that has now ruled for over 300 years, longer than almost any other ruling house worldwide. It has been reported that the 11th surah of the Koran inspired him, where it says that 'He it is, who created the heavens and the earth in six Days – and His Throne was over the waters – that He might try you, which of you is best in deeds.'

Part of the 22-acre area does in fact jut out over the sea. 300,000 square metres of concrete and 40,000 tonnes of steel were used by the French construction company to protect it from the effects of breakers or even earthquakes, as our headscarfed guide explains in flawless English, escorting us through the building. She has more grand figures for us: it is 200 metres long, 100 metres wide, and 60 metres high, and with the forecourt offers space for over 100,000 worshippers. Its façades are covered with 25,000 tonnes of marble, travertine and granite. Its minaret has a cross-section of 25 square metres and rises 200 metres into the sky. At night a laser beam points the way to Mecca from the largest of the three golden balls at the top of the minaret. The three balls are highly characteristic of mosques in this country. The beam can be seen 35 kilometres away, she says. The inside is, if anything, even more impressive, although it does seem to us a little soulless, like an empty museum. Apparently nothing was too expensive for the builder and his French architect

– from the five-acre floor that can be heated from below, the gigantic marble carpet, cedarwood carvings, and the 50 chandeliers of Murano glass, to the *zelliges* and the 1,100 tonne roof that can be opened electronically when the weather is fine. An elegant hammam and dozens of marble lotus flowers that constantly spout water from their blossoms provide over 1,000 worshippers with the opportunity to carry out their ablutions at the same time.

35,000 workers and craftsmen were engaged for six years in its colossal construction. Who paid them? 'The construction,' we hear, 'cost five billion dirhams (around 300 million pounds). By far the largest amount was donated by the population.' We don't hear how the interior minister Driss Basri drummed up the budget in 1987 in only two weeks. Public sector employees had part of their monthly salary docked. Freelancers paid via their associations, and businessmen were ordered to transfer certain sums by governors. And woe betide the subject who refused to pay! Traders, craftsmen and café owners, as a friend later tells us, all dutifully displayed the certificates in their windows that confirmed their 'donation'.

Seaside snapshots

Towards Agadir along the Atlantic coast

Travelling south along the coast from Tangier, we drive through green, sparsely populated land, sometimes flat and marshy, sometimes undulating. The sandy beaches are pencil straight and practically empty. Here and there children are watching sheep and cows, and farmers are laboriously working their fields, even using wooden ploughs. The first larger town is Asilah. Carthaginian and Roman ships once berthed here. It was occupied by the Portuguese in the 15th century, as almost all the North African harbours were. Later it was twice briefly Spanish. The most interesting tourist sight in the pretty, enwalled medina is the former residence of Abdallah el Raisouli. In the years before, during and after the First World War, the unscrupulous rebel leader made alternate pacts with the French, the Spanish, the Sultan and the German Kaiser Wilhelm. He was also quite famous for a while when he spectacularly took a string of hostages. Since 1978 his Moorish palace, where he ruled as a pasha for a while, has become famous for another reason: every August it hosts an excellent arts festival.

Larache lies 25 miles further south, at the mouth of the Wadi Loukos. It is noted for its excellent tea plantations and is a particularly clear example of the double nature of each of the coastal towns. It is centred on the circular Place de la Libération, around the edge of which are dotted cafés with elegant arcades. Ignoring the burnouses and the Arabic signs, we could just as easily be in Andalusia. That is not surprising, given that the town was the largest port in the Spanish zone at the time of the Protectorate. But as soon as you step through the horseshoe arch of the old Bab el Khemi gate, you are in a real medina again. The elongated market square is a surging mass of people, like any bazaar, and it leads to a classic kasbah. The Spanish cemetery in the south of the town is a place of pilgrimage for lovers of excessive literature. There we find a simple grave under a single cedar, right above the cliff that falls into the sea. On the whitewashed gravestone you can read the scrawled words: 'Jean Genet, 19th December 1910 – 13th/14th August 86'. The place's melancholy and strange desolation fits the world of discontented outsiders that this writer, who was at different times a pupil at a special school, a foreign legionary and a prisoner, preferred to write about in his books.

Of course, the sprawling slum that we wander into next is much more desolate. As far as your eye can see, there are only corrugated iron huts, walls patched together in a makeshift way, rubbish, barefoot children and young men hanging around with nothing to do. This is the other side of Morocco's dazzling, fairytale beauty, and a smaller version of the infamous *bidonvilles*, the large 'tin can towns' on the edge of Casablanca.

A few miles north of Larache lie the ruins of the ancient town of Lixus, which was only rediscovered in the mid-19th century by the German explorer Heinrich Barth. It is claimed to be the site of the legendary garden of the Hesperides, where Hercules stole the famous golden apples. At the lower end of the town, right beside the road, the walled remains can be seen of the extensive pools where fish were farmed and garum produced. Garum was a fish paste in high demand in Rome's delicatessens. On the way up the hill to the temple we pass an amphitheatre, the ruins of thermal baths and houses. Olive trees and cypresses dot the hillside, reminding us of Tuscany or Greece. From the top of the hill we have a splendid view of the valley and the majestically winding Wadi Loukos.

El Ksar el Kebir, a little way upriver, entered history as the scene of the famous Battle of the Three Kings. On 4 August 1578 the Moroccans thwarted the attempt of the Portuguese king Sebastian I and his 30,000 soldiers to conquer the land in the name of the Christian God. The Portuguese king, his ally the deposed sultan al-Mutawwakkil, and Abd al-Malik, the sultan leading the Moroccan forces, all died in the battle, as did 25,000 men. Weakened by the defeat, Portugal also fell to Spain.

The next town on the road towards the capital is Souk el Arba du Rharb. Its name tells us a lot about it. This agricultural town in the Rharb plain near the coast holds a market every Wednesday. Wednesday is the fourth day of the week, and *arba* means four. Again and again in Morocco you will come across market towns whose names include a number such as *tleta*, which is three, for Tuesday; or *tnin* – two, for Monday. These names signal to traders and customers which day is a particularly good one to visit the town.

We quickly pass by Kenitra, an industrial city established by the French near the mouth of the Wadi Sebou. It was originally named Port Lyautey in honour of their first Resident-General. It is most well known today for its infamous high-security prison and the nearby US air force and navy bases. South of this heavily populated area of little interest to tourists, an amazing sight greets us: we are crossing groves that look almost like a park, there are pines, cork oaks, eucalyptuses, acacias and pear trees. Mamora Forest, we read in a guide book, covers over 400 square miles and was originally planted to counter the damage caused by overgrazing. By the side of the road, boys are selling fresh truffles and bags of walnuts, not to mention living turtles and even foxes.

We drive south. After skirting the Rabat-Mohamme-dia-Casablanca conurbation and passing Azemmour, with its painterly medina above the mouth of the Wadi Oum er Rbia (the 'mother of spring' river), we reach El Jadida. Under its Portuguese name Mazagan, this harbour town was an important link in the chain of fortifications that the Portuguese built along the coast of north-west Africa in the 16th century, thus securing their trading route to India. Although they lost most of these ports relatively quickly to the new great power, the Saadians, who were pushing north from the Draa Valley, they held Mazagan for over 250 years. When its fall was inevitable, they blew up a large part of the mighty citadel, which had been constructed according to the most modern methods of fortification. In the early 19th century it was rebuilt and given its present name, El Jadida, meaning 'the new'.

Following the advice of all the travel guides, we visit the underground cistern in the Cité Portugaise. Built in 1541, and only rediscovered by chance in the 20th century, it certainly has a charm all its own. Its grand, ribbed vaults in a late Gothic style arch over 10,000 square feet. They are reflected in the water along with the two dozen supporting pillars, all covered by algae. Only the quiet and echoing sound of dripping breaks the silence. The Portuguese used the cistern as a fencing school in dry periods. Orson Welles filmed key scenes of his *Othello* here. A few steps away a minaret towers up on the foundations of an earlier, polygonal lighthouse. It is the Muslim world's only minaret with five sides.

A ten-minute drive past El Jadida takes us to the bay of Jorf Lasfar. The port's monstrous industrial complex rises up in front of us: congeries of warehouses as tall as tower blocks, massive vats, cranes and loading ramps, meshed together with high voltage lines, conveyer belts and rail tracks. The Plain of Khouribga, that stretches from Casablanca to Marrakech, holds 40 per cent of the world's phosphate reserves. 25 million tonnes are exported every year, a considerable proportion of that via Jorf Lasfar. The income generated is something of a consolation for a country that has none of its own petroleum and, to buy it, has to pay enormous sums to its neighbour Algeria. Not just phosphate, but also its various derivatives are produced in Jorf Lasfar, such as fertilizer and phosphoric acid. It is a blessing for the country's trade balance, but a nightmare for environmentalists. A yellow haze hangs in the air, and the trees and cacti are covered in a sulphuric dust from the huge smokestacks. Even before the area was concreted over and when only a few fishermen lived here, the port had its current name, which means 'the yellow rock'.

By the next bay the horror has passed. For many miles the coastline is barely built on. Its wonderful sandy beaches will no doubt be a gold mine for tourism in the future, but, thankfully for us, aren't yet. They are skirted at times by fertile fields and oyster beds, at times by salt marshes and reeds. Towards Oualidia the coast becomes rocky and steep.

Safi was once Morocco's chief port and is today one of the country's two main centres for ceramics, the other being Fès. We climb the Colline des Potiers, the 'Potters' Hill'. In over 30 potteries here outside the city – where their fires pose less threat – vases, jugs, plates, and the *tajine* dishes with their 'trumpet lids', are produced by the potters working in cooperatives. Turquoise and saffron are popular colours. Berber rugs provide the patterns for their geometrical designs. The special green glazed tiles – green being the colour of the Prophet – are made here, before they are laid on the roofs of all the country's shrines and mosques in the ancient 'over and under' fashion. We are also shown the individual stages of making a pot: first the wedging of the local clay (which is perfect for pottery because of its lime and iron content); then cutting it into pieces by hand; shaping it on the potters' foot-driven wheels; and the three separate firings in hellishly smoking, domed kilns – the biscuit firing, then those for the under-glaze and the coloured glaze. We are also shown the shop and, of course, our resolve crumbles and we end up leaving with bulky packages in our hands. On the roof of the Kechla, an old stronghold that now holds a ceramics museum, we enjoy the panoramic view of the old town. Later we descend to the Portuguese chapel in the heart of the souk. It was created in the 16th century from the chancel of an earlier cathedral. Many keystones can be seen in its stellar vault. We see a Maltese cross, Safi's coat of arms with its three keys to the city gates, and a papal tiara.

In the city's southern districts we pass endless lines of shabby factories. The awful smell reminds everyone that sardines are canned here and fish turned into oil and fish-meal. The fleet of 3,000 Moroccan cutters hauls almost 600,000 tonnes of sardines from the Atlantic every year – not to mention a further 300,000 tonnes of mackerel, anchovy, brace, plaice, cod, squid and shrimp. The coastal waters along the 2,000 miles from Tangier to La Gouera at the Mauritanian border are some of the best fishing grounds in the world. No wonder that encroachment by fishermen from Andalusia and the Canary Islands often puts Rabat at loggerheads with Madrid.

The port of Essaouira presents a much more idyllic picture. The Carthaginians anchored in its harbour over

2,500 years ago, as archaeologists have proven. At food stalls fresh seafood is being grilled and sold to passers-by, who can sit at little wooden tables to eat it. Not far off, shipbuilders are working on skiffs in little shipyards. What with all the colourful boats along the mole, the fishing nets, the rugged rocks along the coast, the breakers and the screaming seagulls circling elegantly in the stiff breeze, you could almost imagine you were in Normandy or Brittany. Although they were never as successful at trading gold, slaves and ivory.

The old town also has a curiously European feel to it, thanks to a certain Théodore Cornut. This French architect was imprisoned and then commanded by the sultan of the time to fortify the port of Mogador, as the town was then known. The result is a medina with straight streets meeting at right angles, unique in the Arab world and a kind of Moroccan St Malo. Strolling from the harbour towards the town, we pass through the Porte de la Marine, the sea gate built in a classical style. On a broad square nice cafés and restaurants tempt us to linger under their shady trees. To the left the path goes up a ramp and onto the Skala de la Kasbah – the ramparts adorned with a long row of bronze cannons. Underneath in what were once munitions stores, fine craftsmen have set up workshops. Using the thuya and acacia root wood, but also lemon and cedar wood, with mother of pearl, and copper and silver wire, they create the marquetry that Essaouira has been famed for since antiquity, and that is applied to every imaginable object and sold in the town's many souvenir shops and galleries.

Near an interesting museum of traditional art and heritage, we discover a memorial plaque. It declares that the French governor held the young Charles Foucauld under house arrest here in 1884. He was the Catholic priest who later lived in the Sahara for 16 years as a hermit among the Tuareg people of the Ahaggar region. The dictionary that he compiled of their Berber language is the still the best there is. Near to the town's eastern wall, we come across a remarkably classy art gallery. Its owner proudly lets us know that it regularly exhibits works by the country's most important contemporary artists. Essaouira has been the favourite haunt of Moroccan artists and writers since the 19th century. The Purple Islands lie just off the coast of Essaouira. During the reign of the Berber king Juba II they were famed throughout the Roman empire for the workshops that produced a precious purple dye. Today they are a bird sanctuary. The apparently never-ending sandy beach to the south of the town is a favourite spot for surfers. Nestling in white dunes, you will find the little Berber village of Diabat. Hippies flocked here in the 1970s. Among the *kif*-smoking dropouts was a certain Jimi Hendrix, who lived here for five years. One of the songs he wrote here was inspired by the unusual ruins of an old palace on the beach. They were gradually sinking out of sight: 'Castles Made Of Sand'.

The further south we go from here, the more sparse vegetation becomes. The average annual rainfall here is below the psychologically important 400 mm level. Crops are meagre and fields stony. We see more and more camels as we drive on. Some pull a plough, others are loaded with firewood. Gnarled, thorny trees line the road. Daring goats teeter in the treetops high above the ground, nibbling leaves and posing for the tourists who drive by. We are in argan country: the argan is an amazing tree that only grows in this south-west corner of Morocco. Its various products support the local Berbers in many ways. Many people along the road are selling cans of an oil pressed from the stones of the tree's small, yellowish fruit. We later hear that this oil is not only good for the digestion, but is also used by the local people in traditional skin care, as well as being highly valued as a medicine and to treat wounds. A short detour into the interior leads us along a windy little road to Imouzzer des Ida Outanane. The stunning vista of olive groves and flowering almond trees on the mountainsides lives up to the Berber name for the area: 'valley of paradise', in particular at this hour, when the slanting rays of the setting sun gild the trees. At the end of the valley we stop off at a waterfall that everyone's told us about – it is indeed incredibly picturesque. Back on the coastal road, we soon see a multitude of lights from the wide Bay of Agadir. This 'gateway to the south' welcomes hordes of visitors flown in from cold Europe with bright, Moroccan sunshine – for 330 days a year, as the tourist brochures' statistics proudly trumpet.

Among acrobats, storytellers and poets

The magic and mayhem of the Jemaa el Fna

No question about it – the first place you head for in Marrakech has to be the Jemaa el Fna. This is the square where executions were still carried out at the beginning of the 20th century and the skulls of the criminals displayed on stakes; and where today scarcely less exotic spectacles can be seen, although thankfully less bloodthirsty. Is there any other place in Marrakech where the essence of the city is revealed as powerfully? It is all here: its sense of fun, its mystery, its sensuality, its changeability and its anarchic energy.

We have agreed to meet Ahmed Zaidane Lasry late in the afternoon. Eager to begin to soak in the atmosphere, we turn up a bit early and join the crowd of curious onlookers, of locals out for an evening stroll and pickpockets. The tourists, snapping away with flashbulbs, look oddly timid, and do their utmost not to lose sight of their group. Berber farmers have come to town from the south, the Sous and the High Atlas. They will trade goods, find some entertainment far from the village's hard daily life, or let the fortune-tellers advise them on matters of the heart and the healers cure their aches and pains.

And last but not least we have the awe-inspiring protagonists of the ongoing show – the storytellers, soothsayers, clowns, musicians and acrobats. We watch the *charmeurs de serpent* as they hypnotise their snakes with the bagpipe-like melodies of their *ghaita*, and we cast a happy eye over the stallholders' beautiful wares. We watch the fire-eater light his spirit-soaked breath, the artistes form a human pyramid, and the trainers patiently repeat their attempts to coax their monkeys with sugar cubes into performing tricks. Yet the most fascinating of all of them are the storytellers. Two in every three Moroccan women, and half of all men, can't read or write. Even nowadays, most of the audience is lapping up the tall tales with rapt amazement, as if they were the words of an oracle. Every time one of these last guardians of an oral tradition pulls people into an imaginary circle, the *halqa*, with an exciting story (whether of the smutty or sacred variety), they are putting one over their toughest competitor: television. They even manage to captivate us unbelievers who can't understand a single word.

There is no let-up in the jostling, pushing and pulling. Little boys are always thrusting out plates with an insistent look in their eyes. The audience has to pay what's due! It sometimes seems as if little hands are checking to see how secure the button is on the pocket that holds my wallet.

At five o'clock we finally meet Ahmed at the entrance to the Café de France. 'The Jemaa el Fna is *the* sensation in our city,' Ahmed says, once the customary embraces, kisses and complements have been exchanged. He knows what he's talking about. He earned his first dirhams on the square when he was just a whippersnapper, performing tricks and selling trinkets. Since then he has become rich in the tourist business. By nature he's not easily ruffled, but he feels strongly that these ten acres of open space between the Koutoubia Mosque, the medina and the royal palace are the unique heart of his city, the pulse that excites both Marrakchis and foreigners. 'Many friends of mine,' he says, 'who have known the Jemaa el Fna as long as I have, complain that it has been tamed and ruthlessly commercialised. They have good reason to say that – just look at those water sellers!' He points to two old men in fiery red costumes, adorned with copper bells, brass cups and goat's skins. 'They aren't quenching anybody's thirst, they just pose for photos.' And I hear that the young gnawa musicians barely know the traditional ecstatic songs, they just rattle their bells and hold out their cowry-covered hats. The snake-charmers have also pulled out their cobras' poisoned fangs and only play their nasal sounding instruments for show. Monkey trainers, henna painters and the Polaroid portrait photographer, not to mention the men who belly dance in women's clothing – they are all, sighs Ahmed, newcomers here. Without any tradition, real ability or a whiff of spirituality, all they are after is filthy lucre.

There weren't as many attractions before, he remembers, but there were more real masters. Ahmed tells us that the two or three storytellers would attract crowds of hundreds with their yarns. People all over the country knew of the donkey who understood everything his master said. But those greats are gone, the legendary acrobatic cyclist too and the crazy *majdubs*, who in their trances could drink boiling water and walk or lie on splinters of glass.

Admittedly, the modern era has brought some improvements. 'Nowadays you're not running any real risk when you try a speciality – like chickpea soup, sheep's brain, snails or grasshoppers – from one of the mobile food stalls. The authorities are very strict on hygiene.' In fact, everything here that gives a charmingly chaotic impression is actually extremely well organised. The governor has a map of the area on the wall of his office. It pinpoints the exact location of everybody's (highly desired and highly priced) allotted plot. The authorities sell licences, charge monthly rents and check sellers' wares, so that the amount of tat and plastic doesn't get out of control.

The second part of what should be on every new arrival's programme awaits us the next morning: the classic sights of the city. First a whirlwind tour of Moroccan folk art in the Dar Si Said museum, a late 19th century palace in the Alawite style, where we inspect the furniture, rugs, weapons, pottery, jewellery and clothing. The exhibit that lodges most firmly in the memory is a magical ride for children, a kind of big wheel in miniature. It is about 15 feet tall and completely wooden. Its gondolas are made of washtubs. The nearby Dar el Bahia was once the Grand Vizier's palace and it is an appropriately sumptuous riot of faience, marble, stucco, mirrors and cedarwood. A homely place to live? Not likely. It was here that Alfred Hitchcock filmed *The Man Who Knew Too Much* and where Nastassja Kinski stretched languidly on soft cushions for *Harem*.

The Saadian tombs are much more impressive. The necropolis was created just before 1600 and later walled off by Moulay Ismail, the founder of Meknès, with the intention of wiping the dynasty from the people's memory. It was only in 1917, over 200 years later, that the graves were rediscovered. Even today there is an air of enchantment here. The two grandly decorated mausoleums convey a good idea of the wealth that the Saadians accumulated, partly from plundering Timbuktu and partly from trading gold, slaves and sugar with the tribes who lived south of the Sahara. Moulay Ismail had more success in removing the secular monuments to his hated predecessors. Not much is left of the El Badi Palace, built by the Saadian sultan Ahmed al-Mansour and in its day the most grandiose palace in the whole of the Maghrib. Most of the building materials were put to new use in Meknès.

We too had been dealt a rough hand by fate the previous evening. A boy on the Jemaa el Fna had latched onto us. And as he, of course, just happened to have friends where we were from, and wanted to give us letters for them, it took us many energy-sapping arguments to convince him to leave us in peace. This afternoon we take a preventative measure and hire one of the official guides. They can be recognised by their elegant white jellabas, beige *babouches*, wine red fezzes and the copper placard swinging from their necks. Thanks to our guide we are off-limits for the 'illegals'. And as we made a point, right at the start, of explaining that we had no interest in buying ceramics, carpets or brass ornaments, and that he would be paid well enough without any commission, we were finally able to just 'medina' – to stroll, browse, smell and listen unhindered by any unwelcome interruptions.

The souks of Marrakech are not an unfathomable maze like those of Fès, they are more clearly laid-out and more colourful and easygoing. Not that they are much smaller. Without a guide we would still manage to get lost. As it is, we see all the markets pretty systematically. The dyers' market, for example, called the Souk des Teinturiers, is adorned with poppy-red, saffron and indigo bundles of wool that are hung out on drying lines. At the felt-makers' market, the Souk des Lebadiyne, some master craftsmen still knead prayer mats soaked in black soap. The Souk Quessabine's shops sell spices, dried fruits and basketry, sheltered from the sweltering sun by reed awnings. The Souk Smarine is for textiles and clothing. We walk through the *babouche* makers' souk, and coppersmiths', jewellers' and leatherworkers' souks. In the La Criée dark passageway we witness the daily auction of old carpets, burnouses and jellabas. On the Place Rahba Kedima slaves from sub-Saharan Africa were sold off up until 1912. Now it is full of stalls selling snail soup and wool, and of itinerant pharmacists. In addition to all manner of herbs, powders and potions that help against everything from fear to tape worms and impotence, they hawk various items to protect you from, or to work *silhacen*, the infamous black magic. Only at Souk Larzal, the second-hand market for women's undergarments, are our efforts to enter in vain. Two guards bar our way. Foreign men have no business being here! Which is pretty much the truth of the matter.

Down a side alley, we find a particularly charming little shop window belonging to a hairdresser's. As proof that the hairdresser is also a dab hand as a dentist, his window displays a large jar with hundreds of pulled teeth. A cupping glass and a small, strangely shaped pair of scissors indicate that, if needs be, he also works as a healer and circumcises boys.

Later that evening we find ourselves again drawn to the Jemaa el Fna by its bewitching magnetism. The heat of the day has given way to a refreshing coolness. The grill stalls are in place and the coals lit. They and the actors' carbide lamps create cosy islands of light in the crowded darkness. Sitting on a wooden bench in the flickering half-light, spooning up my *harira* (chickpea soup), and munching on a *khobz*, a delicious warm flat bread, I start to think about how many assaults this square has already suffered from our uncontrolled, so-called modern times – and how many it has resisted. In the 1960s and 1970s the local buses all stopped at a bus station in its north-eastern corner. The station was taken elsewhere. Various kiosks and drinks stalls popped up. They had to go too. Just a few years ago its dirt surface, that had been stamped down over the generations by millions of leather slippers and bare feet, was tarmacked over on the occasion of a GATT conference. That meant it lost a little of its earthy anarchy, but it lost none of its vitality and ability to either reject or take in foreign bodies. Even the tourist coaches that, because what they carry is too lazy to walk a few yards, beach like whales on the shores of this sea of people, are soon wrapped in the square's invisible web and neutralised with its juices. Recently, however, worrying news has been heard around the square. A 60-foot high, glass-fronted department store, with its own underground garage, is planned beside the square. Resistance to the idea is growing. Yet, bent over my soup I still catch myself thinking: how much longer will this fairy tale kingdom of circles and words exist?

An oasis of luxury and fashions

A journey through Marrakech's green outskirts

A suitable way to explore the city is in one of the delightfully old-fashioned carriages. Protected from the sun by a black, probably slightly tatty hood, you will roll down the tangled alleys of the medina and along the Ville Nouvelle's wide avenues, rather as if you were in a gondola. The standard route is the *tour des remparts*, taking you as advertised along an eight-mile circuit around the whole medina, along its mighty rammed earth ramparts that are in places a rusty red, and in others ochre. We've hired our *calèche* on the Place de la Liberté and are following the classic route: from roundabout to roundabout, from one town gate to the next. From the Bab Doukkala, in front of which lepers once lived who had been cast out of the town, and where today long-distance coaches pick up passengers, we bob across to the Bab el Khemis. In its shade local farmers sell their livestock every Thursday. We pass the Bab Debbagh, where on the banks of the weak and dirty Wadi Issil tanners have been preparing their hides for as long as people can remember, before driving past the large cemetery and through the Bab Ahmar. This leads us into the labyrinthine courtyards of the *mechouars* in front of the king's palace.

Haggling over the fee before the trip, we agreed with our driver that we would also take in a little of the Palmeraie, the palm groves that can't help but remind every new arrival that Marrakech was founded at a desert oasis, and that this country has its roots in the desert. The name Morocco comes from the Spanish word Marruecos, which was their name for the city of Marrakech. In the Palmerie's 46 square miles there are over 150,000 date palms, or 'burning sons of the earth and Africa's sun', as André Chevrillon once called them. That is now only half as many as a few decades ago. Some look rather decrepit. Recent droughts and the growing population's need for wood have taken their toll on the palms.

It was thanks to Ali ben Youssef that the oasis was extended. The son of the town's founder Youssef ben Tachfine, he constructed an intricate system of aqueducts to provide water for the Haouz plain that Marrakech lies on. These form an underground network of channels, called *khettaras*, that collect and carry the surface and ground water to the fields. As they are underground, very little water is lost to evaporation. Travelling between the palms, we keep on seeing round mounds of earth that have been dug out of the shaft holes; they mark the path of the tunnels. The highest peaks of the High Atlas shine in the distance, like a strange hallucination. Their snow-covered summits supply water to this green, shady paradise down in the valley – even in the heat of summer.

To round things off we are driven through Hivernage and Gueliz, the new town's two elegant districts. When Morocco became a French protectorate in 1912, Marshal Lyautey, the first Resident-General, made a far-sighted decision. Other colonialists had often tried to re-model old towns according to their architects' Western plans, often disfiguring them. He ordered new European districts to be built, but always outside of the city walls. This enabled all the country's historical town centres – whether in Fès, Meknès, Rabat, Safi or Taroudannt – to retain their own architectural and social structures. At the same time the French civil servants could live in modern districts that met all their needs for creature comforts.

Marrakech's medina was spared too. Yet this city, the 'pearl that Allah threw over the Atlas mountains', had always had its own special role to play. Anatole France had in the same year of 1912 dared to make the journey south to this former capital. There was no railway or a road he could take. Once back in Paris, he enthused about its glories. Suddenly Marrakech became a magnet for the smart set. Affluent Americans and French in particular came to pass the winter here in the warm. They built mansions surrounded by magnificent gardens. Many of these villas are in Hivernage, which looks a little Californian. The old exclusivity can certainly still be felt. We roll down avenues full of the intoxicating scent of the orange trees and jacarandas behind which the international jet set has hidden their dream houses. To think that we are only a few minutes from the Jemaa el Fna! There are also any number of luxury hotels and night clubs here, as well as a casino. Gueliz, on the other hand, is the heart of the colonial Ville Nouvelle, the district of banks, boutiques, restaurants and cafés. This is where people come to stroll and shop, where you see the offices of airlines and car rental companies.

Our carriage journey ends in the north-east of Gueliz, at one of Marrakech's most magical hidden corners: the Jardin Majorelle. The painter Jacques Majorelle built himself a villa here in the 1920s, calling it Bou Saf Saf. It is a daring combination of art deco and elements of Moroccan style. After Majorelle's death, Yves St Laurent, the master of exotic haute couture, bought the property. Some of his family's roots were in the Maghrib and he once confessed that it was Morocco that opened his eyes to the possibilities of colour: 'The shadows on the ground and the sand, but also the different shadings in the streets; the women with their turquoise and mauve kaftans – and then this sky!' He renamed it Villa Oasis, painted the artist's studio a cobalt blue so bright that your eyes can't really take it in, and installed a wonderful little museum for Berber arts and crafts. He also opened the garden to the paying public. It is a place of both breathtaking opulence and ascetic silence – an Elysium, flourishing with well-kept bougainvillaea, bamboos, banana trees and hundreds of botanical rarities, broken up here and there by deep-blue pools. Their water lilies and goldfish invite a contemplative mood.

Later that evening we find ourselves in another dream: dining in Dar El Yacout. Marrakech has a wealth of top-class gourmet restaurants – for example, the Dar Mounia and the Trattoria di Giancarlo in Gueliz, or the Stylia in the medina. Monsieur Mohamed Zkhiri's Yacout is one of the finest – and most expensive – of all of them. It is housed in the 18th century palace of a *kaid* (a local governor) and its several, over-lapping floors add immeasurably to its charms. The patio with its pool, the salon for aperitifs, and the dining rooms are all lit with many hundreds of candles in brass candelabras. The carpets are strewn with rose petals and the damask tablecloths are decorated with pomegranate stones. Wherever you look, precious ceramics, carvings and brass ornaments can be seen. Graceful waiters in pure white jellabas serve *couscous d'agneau* from silver dishes, so tender it falls apart when you look at it. I've never seen lamb carved so artistically. Three gnawa virtuosos magic otherwordly rhythms out of their *gembri*, *darbuka* and castanets. The music is similar to what we heard in Tangier and on the Jemaa el Fna, admittedly in a rather different setting. We are invited onto the roof terrace for coffee, where we lounge on carpets and plump cushions. Below us are the lights of the city, above us the heavens and, in the distance, snow on the Atlas mountains shimmers in the moonlight. Let's not wake up quite yet!

Barren lands and iron dogmas

A spin in the High Atlas

Our trip takes us towards Tizi n Test, the more westerly of the two passes over the ridge of the High Atlas. The road here is lined with heavily watered orchards. We see many small watermills for grinding corn. We reach Asni, a pretty market town where Berbers from the mountains and people from the Haouz plain come to trade with each other. Here we turn off into a narrow side valley. The bumpy road leads past hamlets of an almost unimaginable simplicity. The walls of the one-storey houses and stables are made of layers of rammed earth and their flat roofs are of tree trunks and branches, the gaps tamped closed with mud. The windows are tiny; this gives some protection from the extremes of heat and cold. Little terraced fields cling to the steep hillsides. Their bright green is misleading: the crops have been wrestled from the barren land with the utmost effort.

Driving into Imlil, the village that guards the end of the valley, we pass an idyllic oak grove. Dozens of mules have parked themselves in the shade of the trees. A mule can be hired with an officially licensed guide to the area, an *accompagnateur*, for 250 dirhams per day. Imlil is attracting more and more Europeans, who use it as a starting point for tours of the mountainous Toubkal National Park. The local tour organisers can offer week-long hiking tours that take you from one remote hut to the next. Jebel Toubkal is 13,670 feet high, the highest peak in the Maghrib. At Oukaimeden in the next valley, winter sports enthusiasts are in heaven. There are comfortable hotels, ski lifts and well maintained pistes. Africa's highest cable car can take passengers up to 11,000 feet. Above Imlil two Irishmen stride towards us. Even in the most remote farms, they complain to us, the children have already learnt how to beg. But the mountains up there, they are really something. They tell us that they saw eagles, vultures, mouflons and boar. Our two mountaineers' faces shine bright red. Northern Europeans can easily underestimate the strength of Morocco's midday sun. After all, we are only 31 degrees latitude from the equator and not much more than 50 miles, as the crow flies, from the Sahara's first dunes.

We drive back towards the main road. Once past Asni, the valley narrows and the air becomes cooler. Far below us the melt waters of the Wadi Nfis burble. In the 19th century Goundafi tribesmen still controlled this strategically important valley pass from their powerful kasbahs on either side of the river. The High Atlas was then known as the 'China of the West'. Unbelievers who penetrated its valleys were risking their lives. The strict attitudes of the local Berbers had, 800 years' earlier, even changed the course of world history ...

Less than an hour by car south-west of Asni, about 20 miles and a good 100 steep serpentine bends before the Tizi n Test pass, we reach what was the epicentre of the political upheaval – the little village of Tin Mal. It was here at this remote spot that a certain Ibn Tumart established a *ribat*, a fortified monastery, around 1120. He planned to topple the Almoravid dynasty. By his religious understanding, they were grossly decadent and worldly. Islam too, he thought, had been defiled by humanising the idea of God and adding all kinds of mystical rituals. Promising to purify Islam, he declared himself the Mahdi, the long awaited last prophet. He rallied the local tribes around him, uniting them in a strictly hierarchical society, and declared Holy War, *jihad*, on the political establishment. His moralistic warriors were known as the al-Muwahhidun (the 'Unitarians'), which led to the Spanish term Almohad. Spurred on by his successor Abd al-Mumin, they conquered Marrakech. Soon they were ruling – if only for a century – over a kingdom that encompassed Tunisia, Algeria, Morocco and Muslim Spain. In Tin Mal they erected a mighty mosque in honour of their founder. It is the first great example of the Almohad architecture that later created such landmark buildings as the mosques in Marrakech (the Koutoubia), Rabat (with its Hassan Tower) and even Seville, with the famous Giralda minaret. We remember seeing the ruins of Tin Mal on a trip a few years ago. Since then this historical shrine has been lavishly and sensitively restored. Its defensive, no-frills harshness conveys once again Ibn Tumart's iron dogmas.

In Hollywood's holy land

From Agadir through the Anti-Atlas to Ouarzazate

For three days we've indulged in what every Northern visitor to Agadir does in late winter. We've walked along the miles and miles of beaches, we've sat in deck-chairs sunning ourselves, reading, refusing the hawkers in a friendly but firm manner, we've swum briefly in the Atlantic – it is only 17 degrees Celsius, and feasted on freshly caught fish every evening before strolling along the main street to the accompaniment of music from the clubs. We are happy to see clean streets and relatively tastefully built hotels and do our best to ignore the signs wooing tourists in all languages. On our fourth day there we are hit by the restlessness that such mass tourist resorts tend to cause. We take off, south-west into the mountains.

The first quarter of an hour dampens our spirits. We are stuck in a line of lorries and shared, inter-city taxis. The little stretch between Inezgane and Ait Melloul is the most congested in the country. It's here that two trunk roads meet – one from the deep south, from Tiznit, Tan Tan and Laayoune, and the other which connects the coast with the interior between the Sahara and the High

Atlas. It doesn't help that the rows of soulless new blocks have made both towns heart-rendingly ugly. Not much later we turn off and are saved: our narrow, windy – and empty – road takes us up into an especially breathtaking landscape. It is a highland; it almost seems as wide as those in Scotland. It is bordered by high walls of rock, underneath which archaic villages nestle and imitate the reddish brown of the region. Even the steepest slopes have been terraced and planted with olive trees. *Agadirs*, this Berber region's characteristic fortified granaries, crown many hilltops.

Tafraoute is the hub of this region. The town is in a hollow in the mountains, 4,000 feet above sea level. It doesn't prove to be anything special – it has a nice but provincial bazaar, a souvenir shop and a fancy hilltop hotel that was designed to look like a fortress. The surroundings more than make up for it: there are absolutely bare granite summits reaching up to the sky that is never cloudy. Between them lie groves of palm, almond and olive trees. The area's landmark is the Chapeau de Napoleon, a rock formation that is like a cross between Monument Valley and Meteora without its monasteries, and does actually bare a vague resemblance to the Corsican emperor's tricorne. Looking west, the landscape is dotted with huge contorted boulders – woolsacks made of granite and polished by wind and weather – that look as though a giant has scattered them there. Following sandy tyre tracks off the road, we find a group of rocks behind a hillock. They've been painted bright pink and blue. In the early 1980s the Belgian artist Jean Vérame used 20 tonnes of natural paints to create his own personal take on land art. It may sound rather pretentious, but it is an impressive sight to see.

However, the most stirring scenery awaits us in the Valley of Ammeln. The villages of the Ammeln, a Shluh Berber tribe, hang on the sides of a towering mountain, Jebel Lekst. It is over 7,500 feet tall and its fissured sides glow different colours. Depending on the light that hits them, they change from a light ochre to red or violet. Below them are sprawling palm groves. Just before Oumesnat, the valley's largest village, a hand-painted sign beside the road indicates the way to a *maison berbère typique*. Our curiosity gets the better of us. After a ten-minute walk through fields and up steep alleys, a blind old man welcomes us. He's been waiting in the shady porch of a three-storey house for visitors, among them no doubt a good many coachloads from Agadir. The house's walls are stone at their base, and above that *pisé*, a rammed mixture of earth and straw. Argan wood and palm fronds were used for the ceilings. The old man starts the tour, not attempting to hide the routine nature of it. The ground floor is both stables and work space. It contains three millstones, 'Moulinex berbères' he calls them with a smirk. There is one for corn, one for henna, spices and coffee, and one for extracting argan oil. We hear that women collect the indigestible argan stones from goat droppings. They need two and a half kilos of stones for a litre of oil. Each litre takes four days to produce, the price is 100 dirhams. Upstairs we are shown all sorts of old everyday objects: traps for porcupines, gazelles and foxes, wooden locks and keys, hand-embroidered *babouches*, adults' sleeping mats woven from palm leaves, and the piles of straw that children sleep on. Confusing characters are written on a piece of paper on the wall. They are the letters of the Tifinagh alphabet, the Tuareg people's alphabet. The Tuareg are the only Berbers who write their language in their own script. Many of the numerous Berber dialects are only oral, others use Arabic or Latin characters when they write. Today, our guide laments, only poor people live in traditional houses like this – 20 per cent of the villagers at most. Anyone who can afford to, builds a modern cement house on the edge of the village. Most young men have left for the cities anyway.

West of Tafraoute more phenomenal vistas open up. From the Col du Kerdous we can see the coastal plain spread out below us. Not long afterwards we take a left turn to the *zaouia* of the 16th century holy warrior and mystic Sidi Ahmed ou Moussa. A central figure in southern Morocco's spiritual and political history, he is highly revered as a holy man. He resisted the Portuguese, who were pushing inland from the Atlantic, and worked with missionary zeal for a renewal of Sufism. He also established a brotherhood of archers and acrobats. As with other charismatic Moroccan leaders, his tomb is in the middle of a large cemetery. It is similar to the Idrisid tombs in Fès and Moulay Idris. It is quadrangular, with a glazed green roof, and crystal chandeliers hang above the sarcophagus that is draped in a green sheet. Pretty stucco and *zellige* decorate the room. Here there are also ostrich eggs swinging from a roof beam – an indication of the survival of some animistic beliefs. Even the outward appearance of the women on duty at the tomb suggests they are particularly pious. Their haiks, the cloth wraps that are normally brightly coloured, are black. They also wear black hijabs and they make a point of turning away when we look their way by chance. At the foot of the long flight of steps down from the *zaouia* are several market squares and any number of little bazaar areas. They are empty, all the shops are closed. Three times a year, we hear, *moussems* resembling enormous country fairs are held here in honour of the wise master. Southerners who are too poor to make the pilgrimage to Mecca instead attend the largest *moussem*, which is held at the end of each summer.

Near Tiznit, a town with rich mercantile and crafts traditions, we join the main coastal road again. If we fancied endless hours driving through a monotonous landscape of salt pans, sand dunes and loose stones, we could just carry straight on south for 350 miles to Laayoune, the capital of the province of Western Sahara. Indeed, if we transferred to a Land Rover that was ready for the desert, we could head down another 600 miles to the border with Mauretania at La Gouera, escorted by the military from Dakhla onwards. But we manage to resist temptation. Instead we choose to turn back to Agadir, where we can strike out east on the legendary 'Kasbah Trail'.

The provincial capital of Ouarzazate is on a 4,000 foot high desert plateau. It is here that the west-east road from Agadir to Er Rachidia crosses the north-south road from Marrakech to Zagora. Our first spin around town doesn't prove particularly edifying. Most of the town is new, and bland. All the administrative buildings, souvenir shops, supermarkets and petrol stations have been lined up along an overlarge avenue, which – like all of Morocco's cities' main streets – is called Mohammed V. Behind the shops the usual concrete blocks of housing spread out without any apparent design. Ouarzazate was founded 70 years ago by the French as a garrison town for their Foreign Legion. For a long time it struggled on as a miserable outpost. The late 1970s heralded the start of its boom years, when organised tourism arrived. Since those days it has been used by tour organisers as the starting point for tours into the desert and mountains. South-east of the so-called town centre, an extensive hotel district has been built from nothing. Its hotels are all four- or five-star and have a total of over 5,000 beds. Unfortunately, the planned nature of the district is all too obvious.

Over on the western edge of town, another sight rises above the bare plain, half-hidden behind tall wooden boards. It is a Far Eastern temple, complete with colourful roof tiles, a carved dragon's head on the ridge of the roof and bright red beams. We want to solve this mystery. But at the gate to the site we are rudely shooed away. 'No access!' A short battle of words later and we know a little more: we have found film studios. The Chinese temple we saw is a left-over from the mid-1990s, when Martin Scorsese filmed *Kundun* here, the Dalai Lama's story. After having heard this, we actually do start to find the majestically wide landscape and clear light rather Tibetan. In the lobby of the largest hotel in town, the Bel

Air, we later find a faded sheet of paper with instructions for a film crew. We read that the scene 'David reads the Psalms' was planned that day for the film *Davide*. David and the extras – Uriah's soldiers and the 'crowd' – were to be on set by 6:50 prompt. The receptionist tells us that an Italian team spent several years in the area, filming a series about the Old Testament for American television. Especially in the 1990s, Ouarzazate was the 'Hollywood of the Maghrib'. The sheet has been left up as a souvenir.

Why this place? The local film-producer Jimmy Ahmed Abounoum tells us one evening over a glass of tea. 'Directors and stage designers found here, and sometimes still find, the archaic buildings that they need for many films. That saves them the trouble and cost of building huge stage sets.' In addition, there is an almost constant supply of good weather. It almost never rains. But the main attraction is the fantastic light. 'The air,' he raves, 'is absolutely clear from sunrise to sunset. That gives the landscape such bright colours, this unique ochre in its infinite shades.' A number of major projects in the 1980s brought rapid expansion to Ouarzazate: the James Bond film *The Living Daylights*, *The Jewel of the Nile* starring Kathleen Turner and Michael Douglas, and Bernardo Bertolucci's film version of Paul Bowles' book *The Sheltering Sky* were all filmed here. Jimmy remembers how one of his jobs on *Kundun* was to find Moroccans who looked like Tibetans. Morocco doesn't yet have specialist agencies for that – apart from one that charges an arm and a leg. It had never been too difficult to find Semitic-looking extras for the usual biblical films. But Tibetans ... 'It wasn't easy, but I worked it out. Around 1950, just before France pulled out of its protectorate in Indochina, many Moroccans were fighting there too. When Paris banished our Mohammed V to Madagascar, they deserted and fought for the Vietcong.' Quite a few of them married Vietnamese women and returned home with their new families in 1972. Most of them opened Vietnamese restaurants. 'Those were my people.'

The backdrop for many films' biblical scenes is the Kasbah Taourirt, on the road out of town into the Dades Valley. It was the residence of one of the Glaoui chiefs. The Glaoui are a Berber clan who accumulated significant wealth and influence during the Protectorate era by collaborating with the French. Naturally, after independence in 1956 they fell into disgrace and lost their privileges. Taourirt is considered one of the largest and most beautiful of the Berber fortresses. Well over 1,000 people once lived in this highly defendable warren of streets, courtyards, interconnected housing units and common areas. In fact, it housed all the members of a tribe, as well as many Jews in their own quarter. Today no more than a fraction of the lavishly restored kasbah is occupied. The chief's residence, including his prayer room, harem and dining room, are now open to the public as a museum.

Another corner is occupied by the office of the Centre for the Maintenance and Restoration of Southern Morocco's Architectural Heritage. 'There are complex social reasons behind the dramatic decline of most kasbahs,' we are told by the office's director, the sociologist Ait el Kaid M'barek, himself a descendent from the Draa Valley of a *kaid*, a kind of provincial governor. 'These constructions have, like medieval European castles, lost their original functions in many different ways. They no longer have a purpose as refuges and food stores, now that Morocco is a centrally controlled nation state and the settled tribes no longer have to defend themselves from attacks by hostile neighbouring tribes or the desert nomads. Nor are they as needed to provide accommodation for whole clans – every year the social fabric of these clans is coming more and more undone, people want to live in separate little houses.' Added to that, the kasbahs are literally crumbling because many men have left to work in the cities. After the rare but torrential rainstorms, the women and elderly who are still at home cannot repair all the damage to the *pisé* walls. Recently Rabat has taken countermeasures, subsidising the renovation of at least some of the kasbahs.

The Kasbah Ait Benhaddou is, as a whole, an even more impressive example of this kind of archaic earth architecture, that outside southern Morocco can only be found in Yemen. A photographer's dream, it was built on a steep mountain slope high above a river lined with palms, not far from the main road towards Tizi n Tichka and Marrakech. No fewer than six *tighremts* rise above its higgledy-piggledy cubed houses and rusty red walls. They are highly decorated granaries, each with four towers. They were impregnable, as they had almost no windows. No wonder that this location can also be seen in many films, for example in the 1961 film *Sodom and Gomorrah* by Robert Aldrich and Sergio Leone. Yet first impressions are deceptive in this case. Only a handful of families still live in Ait Benhaddou. Many roofs have caved in, ceilings are rotten, streets are full of rubble, and whole buildings have collapsed. Quite a while ago UNESCO added the whole complex to its list of world heritage sites in need of preservation, and it restored parts of it at the time. More extensive work is still needed if the site is to be saved.

52 days to Timbuktu

On the Kasbah Trail towards the Sahara

At Ouarzazate the Kasbah Trail forks. One road heads south-east along the upper reaches of the Draa river, towards the Sahara. The other fork follows the Dades river east, via Boumalne, Tinerhir and Goulmima, until it reaches Er Rachidia. Heeding the desert's call first, we cross a cracked, plant-less pass before coasting down into an absolute dream of a setting. The Draa Valley is a perfect example of a river oasis. It winds for more than 100 miles through a wide canyon. The river is lined by fields, villages, kasbahs and shrines, as well as hundreds of thousands of date palms. It is only March now, but the air blasting in our faces is already as hot as if it were from a hair-dryer. In mid-summer the temperature can rise to almost 50 degrees Celsius.

The cultural highlight of this land that time forgot is Tamegroute, a town surrounded by mighty, embrasured walls. The founder of the Naciri brotherhood, one of the most highly regarded of southern Morocco, is buried here. A library adjoins his mausoleum. Among its 4,000 medieval manuscripts are texts on history, astronomy, medicine and mathematics, as well as Hadiths and Korans. The jewel of the collection is a Koran on gazelle skin parchment from the late 11th century. Anyone can view it.

Reaching the southern end of this dream valley we are a little disappointed. Here, where we lose the Draa in the sand, there is no grand finale, no undulating waves of dunes, high as houses, crashing onto the hem of the inhabited world. No, the Sahara just peters out in a stony, barren plain. Mhamid is the last outpost of civilisation in this direction and has that typical frontier town charm. There's a mosque, a café, a petrol station, two or three shops, including a butcher's, and a collection of low concrete cubes which the settled nomads now call home. Above the butcher's doorway a skinned and disembowelled goat hangs from a hook, glistening in the sun. The desert wind whips up clouds of dust in the streets. Mutts find sheltered corners and sit blinking and yawning. Behind the small town a line of tanks is lurking in wait. Their cannons are trained south, raised and ready for action. They face the hostile nothingness beyond. 'M'sieur, m'sieur, un bonbon, pour moi, un bonbon, m'sieur ... !' Suddenly our car has been surrounded by a screaming horde of children. Tourists seldom make it to Mhamid. In the Draa Valley's main town Zagora, 30 miles earlier, the tarmacked road had ended and we'd seen the famous sign for the caravanserais: '52 days to Timbuktu' had been written in an uneven script. Below a caravan of camels had been painted in a lovely naïve way.

The following day we follow the Dades east from

Ouarzazate. The landscape here has a Biblical feel to it. To the left are the rock walls of the High Atlas, to the right those of Jebel Sarhro. Between them lie a long chain of powerful kasbahs. Ancient Canaan and the time of Sumeria and Assyria all seem to have come alive again. At the bottom of the valley the river weaves along – a meagre vein of life. In the middle of this dusty world of yellow, ochre and brown, our eyes feast on the shining green and golden carpets of the small fields that lie on the banks of the river. They are no bigger than allotment patches and in them the villagers wrestle what they can from the thin soil. They grow potatoes, carrots, wheat, barley and onions for their own consumption. In February the pomegranate and almond trees blossom on the edges of the fields, giving the carpets a pastel pink border.

At the time of the Protectorate, the French divided the occupied territory for agricultural purposes into two parts: the '*Maroc utile*' and '*Maroc inutile*'. The 'useful' part was the fertile plains near the Atlantic. The French worked this land on a large scale, using modern mechanised farming. The rest of Morocco, especially the stony land beyond the Atlas range, was the part that wasn't of use. This area was not modernised. Again and again we come across groups of women cutting the ripe corn by hand, bending low as they work. Here a dromedary is ploughing furrows in a field with a wooden plough. There a man is watching a single cow. Around one of the few bends we have to brake suddenly: a herd of sheep and goats are sauntering across the road. Not even one in every two Moroccan farmers owns his own land.

We are particularly struck by the old men and women who – as in every remote region in North Africa – we see squatting motionless with a bundle or a bag by the side of the road. Are they waiting for a bus? Or a shared taxi? Or are they just there? We will never know.

In places the narrow river oases widen into woods of palm trees and carefully terraced fruit and vegetable gardens, for example at Skoura and Kelaa des Mgouna. On this stretch of the trip the heady, heavy scent of wild roses often assails us through the car's open windows. The region is renowned for its cultivated roses and for its rose petal extracts. When we check into the hotel in Kelaa des Mgouna, the receptionist sprinkles us liberally with scented water. It is early May and according to custom the new harvest has to be celebrated in this wet but cheerful way.

We arrive in Boumalne the next morning just in time for the weekly market. The open square, lined with arcades, is a hive of business activity. Numerous traders have erected tents over themselves and their wares, others have laid large cloths on the ground in front of themselves to mark their stands. Fresh fruit and vegetables are piled next to aromatic mint leaves and barrels of olives. No, there's no reason for people to go hungry here. A good many farmers are waiting with their mules for the black-smith. They need to re-shoe their animals every two to three months. Nearby the cobbler works from his mobile workshop. He cuts rubber for the soles of sandals from the old tyres that he has stacked beside him. Most of the visitors to the bazaar are women – largely Berber women with their self-confident, open faces, but there are also veiled Arab women.

A short drive from Boumalne takes us to the start of one of the country's most spectacular gorges. The Dades has here cut a path through the southern slopes of the Atlas mountains. If you are willing to put up with several hours of bumpy travel, and assuming it doesn't rain, you can wind your way along the steep serpentine road from here up to Imilchil. You will have to drive at almost walking pace. Imilchil is known far and wide for the *moussem* that brings the Ait Hadiddou there every September. According to their ancient custom, girls who are of a marriageable age are lavishly made up (a very photogenic sight), and then offered in marriage (much like sellable commodities).

Near Tinerhir where the region's other famous gorge, the Todra Gorge, emerges from the mountains, a man approaches on a mountain bike. He is fair skinned, and is wearing a skintight, bright jersey. He is going hell for leather, sweating profusely. He is obviously a European. The High Atlas has more than 400 peaks of over 10,000 feet. In recent years it has become popular for adventurous tourists to conquer these peaks one way or another. Not only do the specialist tour operators offer hiking and skiing tours, they now also offer climbing, canoeing and mountain bike tours. There is naturally a certain uneasy feeling at seeing this socially and ecologically fragile system penetrated by pleasure-seeking foreigners. On the other hand, several hundred young Berbers have already been able to gain their qualifications as mountain guides at the tourism college, allowing them to earn money in their home region. This at least slows down the catastrophic flight of young people from this rural region.

Er Rachidia has a local importance as an administrative centre. It has, however, little to interest us and so we turn off the main road at Tinejdad and head for our journey's final destination. The Tafilalet is the largest single oasis region in the country. Its great forest of palms and its sprawling fields are watered for dozens of miles around by two rivers running parallel to each other, the Ziz and the Rheris. This led to the region being dubbed 'Morocco's Mesopotamia'. Vegetables, corn, cotton and tobacco all thrive here, as do the bushes whose leaves are used to make the *henna* that Moroccan women love to adorn their hands, feet and faces with. It was from here that the Alawites, who were originally from Arabia, set out to conquer the Saadian kingdom. Little remains to be seen of the Sijilmassa except a few sorry, earthen ruins. This city at the nexus of Trans-Saharan trade was, it is said, home to 100,000 inhabitants in its heyday between the 11th and 15th centuries. Several hundred *ksours*, or fortified villages, were also part of the city.

We often pass boys at the side of the road who hold out geodes. 'Amethyst, pyrite, manganite ...' they say in broken French if we stop to inspect their sparkling green, red and violet wares. Friends who were a little too trusting tell us that the stones quickly lose their stunning colours if they get wet.

We press on via Erfoud and Rissani. From there the road is a terrible sand and gravel trail all the way to Erg

Chebbi. Finally we are face to face with the Sahara, just as North Europeans romantically imagine it. Dunes tower up above us. Some are 300 foot high. Their curvy ridges have something erotic about them. You can hire a Land Rover here and gun it over the dunes, or have a more lethargic test ride on a dromedary. We are very happy just to watch the eternally unchanging, yet eternally awe-inspiring spectacle of the sun setting and the stars appearing. Tunisia, Algeria and Morocco are called Jazirat al Maghrib in Arabic literature, 'the island of the West'. Of the three seas that surround the island, there is no doubt that the one that fascinates me most is the sea we are standing on the edge of.

Glossary

babouches	Moroccan slippers
darbuka	musical instrument
Fassis	the people of Fès whose families have lived there for many generations
fondouk	hostel for traders
garum	fish paste
gembri	three-stringed lute
ghaita	Arab oboe
gnawa	music which has its roots in sub-Saharan Africa, brought to Morocco many centuries ago by slaves from Ghana, Mali and Nigeria
haik	cloth wraps
harira	chickpea soup
harquus	henna decoration that traditional women have painted on their hands, feet and even faces every few weeks
jellaba	floor-length shirt worn by men as their main upper garment
jinn	evil spirits
kaid	local governor
kasbah	formerly the name of the centre of a town, later it came to denote a fortress

kashruth	Jewish dietary laws
khobz	warm flat bread
kif	hashish
Marrakchi	resident of Marrakech
medina	old centre of a town
mellah	Jewish quarter
mendoub	Sultan's minister
moussem	a pilgrimage followed by a feast
muezzin	he who calls the faithful to prayer
negafa	women who organise weddings
shariah	Islamic law
sharif	one who claims direct descent from the Prophet Mohammed
sheikh	a leader, in particular the chief or head of an Arab or Berber tribe, family or village
souk	market, often covered
surah	verse from the Koran
tighremt	highly-decorated granaries, each with four towers and almost no windows
ulema	Islamic scholars
zaouia	tomb or shrine
zellige	mosaics made of glazed ceramic tiles